<u>Preface</u>

Born into The Trap was conceived out of a burning desire

to combat the lies and false definitions of ghetto life in America.

The ghetto I grew up in was a beautiful place filled with joy and

laughter when violence and poverty weren't directly in the

atmosphere. I learned many great lessons from this

environment, and this wisdom has aided me in having the kind of

life I have today. My hope is, parents of the future generation

can pass these lessons to their children to arm them with the

knowledge needed to erase the false narrative that has been

imprinted on urban America for the past twenty to thirty years.

I write this book not because I wanted to, but mostly

because I feel it is my obligation to help others navigate the

terrible trap known as the ghetto.

I write this book for all the friends I grew up with in

Harlem who wanted a better way but weren't able to figure it out

until it was too late.

I write this book for all those in the ghetto who wondered as I did, "Why was I born into this environment? How can I make it better? How can I improve my life?"

I write this book for anyone who has ever lost a loved one to senseless violence and still does not understand why.

I write this book for the good kid turned killer who killed out of pride and is serving a lengthy prison term, wishing to turn back the hands of time.

I write this book for all the women who wish they could walk down the block without being called a bitch or a hoe.

I write this book for the drug dealer who if he were only shown another way to live comfortably would have made drug dealing his last resort instead of his only option.

I am no superhero or extraordinary person. The tools I used to escape the *TRAP* can be easily duplicated by anyone. It will be a great day in America when young urban youth no longer need to be extraordinary to improve the circumstances they were born into. When it becomes ordinary for urban youth to achieve, America will become an even brighter shining example on a hill. These are the hopes and dreams which have led me to undertake this project.

I'd like to thank all those I grew up with in the ghetto, for good or bad, you all taught me something. You know who you all are—the basketball coaches and elders who steered me in the right direction, my mom for nurturing me in such a challenging environment,, my brother for pushing me to follow my own path, my sisters who always made sure my physical appearance was presentable, and last but not least, my dad for all the advice and forewarnings.

In my opinion, having been able to escape the *TRAP* and not passing on the map would be equivalent to a slave escaping the plantation and not leaving behind the map, so others can do the same

<u>My Miseducation</u>

The Trap was a terrible teacher. It was a figurative classroom decorated with countless untruths, false perceptions, and other damaging lessons that altered the minds of those residing in it.

Right was wrong. Wrong was right.

Good was bad. Bad was good.

The moment my family moved from the Upper West Side to Harlem, I became a student in this distorted learning environment. It did not take me long to realize the brainwashing affect it had on me and those around me.

One night when entering my building with my mom, I overheard two guys talking about a pair of Nike sneakers they described as being "dope." Growing up in the crack era, I had seen many commercials that referred to drugs as "dope", so I wondered why they chose to use such a negative word to describe the sneakers they seemed so in love with. I figured it was simply a cool way of speaking, but soon learned that in the Trap most things were an alternate reality in comparison to the rest of society.

On another occasion, a teenage boy was eating a cheeseburger, and he too used a drug reference to describe the food he was eating. He emphatically stated, "THIS SHIT IS CRACK!" I was again confused as to why he would use such a destructive thing like crack to describe something he enjoyed eating so much.

The cycle of confusion continued one day when a friend jokingly criticized me for pronouncing the word skully (a term for a winter hat) properly. From my perspective, the way I pronounced it was perfectly fine, however in his eyes I was somehow talking funny.

Up until this point, I viewed myself as having a strong New York City accent since I had been an avid fan of rap music for as long as I can remember. Apparently, I had not developed the accent needed to pronounce the word skully incorrectly

enough. This interaction with my friend again magnified the

miseducation and re-education I would undergo for the

remainder of my adolescence and early adult years.

As I gradually absorbed the norms of my neighborhood, I

began to wear my sneakers slightly untied and my baseball hat

tilted to the side. It seemed everything mainstream society did,

we had to put a twist on it by doing the opposite. Another style

developed where we would wear our jeans inside of our socks.

As ridiculous as these styles may come across, they made us feel

cool because we were able to stand out by being different. These

styles indirectly ingrained in me that I was on the outside of the

norms of society. I was not supposed to want to be like "them."

The problem was--As I was learning how not to be like *them,* I

was simultaneously being taught how not to be my true self.

The cartoons we watched exacerbated the issue. The not

so subtle message that black was evil was repeatedly drilled into

our subconscious thoughts. One of my favorite cartoons, *Casper*

The Friendly Ghost was a perfect example. Casper, the good guy, was pure white, and the numerous evil characters either were black or always wore the color black.

I remember thinking to myself—I am not a bad person, and my skin isn't really black. The people who live below 96th Street cannot possibly all be good people, and they do not really have white skin. So, why are they so happy all the time and why are their neighborhoods so nice? Maybe having light skin did automatically make you good.

By this point, I had already been miseducated enough to leave me skeptical about everything I was learning. Even being armed with this level of skepticism did not prepare me for the miseducation I would acquire from my formal schooling.

The lessons taught about slavery prompted many questions. Why were African people chosen out of the billions in the world as a target for slavery? Who were the decision makers that allowed such a horrific thing to happen for so long? How did

these people live before their lives were ruined by such evil?

None of the answers to these questions were being

taught, and I soon realized it was my duty to research the

essence of this disease called racism which has miseducated both

blacks and whites for so many years.

It became clear that the world had truly little sympathy

for people with darker skin.

Even after slavery ended, the mistreatment continued, and even

grew more hateful. Jim Crow Laws, which were technically

relegated to the states below the Mason-Dixon line, were overtly

carried out throughout the entire United States.

Just when I thought the discrimination was only being

carried out in America, I learned about the apartheid system in

South Africa and the caste system in India, as well as other laws

throughout the world which entitled individuals with lighter skin

a greater humanity than people with darker skin.

This is when I came to fully understand why there was such a disparity between black and white people throughout the globe. I then vowed to elevate myself to a higher standard of living than the one I found myself trapped in.

Even with all this information and determination, it took a valiant effort to defend myself against all the misinformation I was being bombarded with.

One of the most glaring pieces of miseducation was the idea that going to jail was a badge of honor. I could not comprehend how being locked in a cage was somehow an accomplishment. It was perhaps a failed attempt to prove that if you could survive prison, you could do anything. Ironically, once you go through that experience of going to jail, society will continue to keep you locked up and allow you to do actually extraordinarily little. It is almost as if you were quarantined from the rest of society. Going to prison was masked as an opportunity to earn stripes in the neighborhood, but when many of my friends were released instead of earning stripes, they were stripped of almost everything. I personally grew allergic to the idea of ever being shackled in chains. After all, I learned about the struggles of slavery. I could not help but ask myself, "Shouldn't black people do everything possible to stay away from shackles and handcuffs?"

It was unfathomable that we could have mentally reverted three hundred years by romanticizing the idea of being held in bondage. In my opinion, if we were going to glorify prison as a badge of honor, we should have all remained slaves.

Throughout the late 1980's and 1990's, the New York City jail population primarily consisted of African American men from just a few neighborhoods. Because of this, there were weekly bus trips to the upstate prisons. Although I understood the joy of seeing family members you had not seen in a long time, it always bothered me that this experience mirrored the energy of an NFL pre-game tailgate party.

There were two locations designated as the pick-up location for transport to the upstate prisons. One directly outside Yankee Stadium in the Bronx and the other at 59th Street and Columbus Circle in Manhattan. The euphoria was generally high. The visitors consisted of mostly women who gathered as early as 4:00 A.M. They wore their best attire and makeup. Their conversations were related to bragging about the crimes their boyfriends were incarcerated for and how much respect their loved one had in the trap. Meanwhile, I would sit on the bus angry that I had to travel five hours to see my best friend who was incarcerated for unnecessarily brandishing a gun during a truly petty altercation. During my three visits to see my friend, I did not see a single Caucasian or Asian. It infuriated me and further magnified how miseducated we were in the African American community. I realized just how far behind we were as a demographic mostly due to the injustice of slavery and Jim Crow laws.

Many of the individuals who were in these prisons more than likely would not have been there if African Americans were compensated for the atrocities committed against our ancestors in the same fashion as other races. This compensation allowed these other communities to restructure. Since these injustices were never rectified, I made a conscious effort to give myself a head start so many others did not have by creating my own reparations.

In essence, I began to create a personal reconstruction since the African American community was never truly reconstructed.

Throughout my time in the Trap, I realized we often valued things that did not necessarily have real value. We basically worshipped clothes, jewels, and cars. One of my favorite pastimes was watching the fancy cars drive past my block heading to the various New York City highways. I mostly hung out on 142nd Street and 8th Avenue which was directly on the route to the famed Rucker tournament that was played across from the Polo Grounds houses.

It was not uncommon to see our favorite entertainers driving past in their luxury vehicles. 8th Avenue was like a stage where all the glitz and glamour happened, especially during the summer.

These constant images created a lust inside of me for my first fast foreign car. My friends would always tease me because I would often talk about having a Range Rover one day. After unlearning all the miseducation, I received over the years, I was able to become a radiology technologist. The savings I had amassed in my first year of working was burning a figurative hole in my pocket. I was somewhat confused as to where I should invest it. Although no one knew exactly how much money I had accumulated, many could sense I had a significant amount of money saved up due to me remaining in the projects where my mom's rent was about $250/month. Their estimations led many to advise me that buying a new car was in my best interest. I steadily searched for things which would allow me to taste the fruits of my labor. I considered buying a Cadillac CTS, but after learning of the exorbitant rates for parking and auto insurance in

Manhattan, it became clear that I must refrain from this impulse.

Also, when I considered the hustlers in my neighborhood—the

ones who drove around in fancy cars but did not have any real

assets—I veered even further from the impulse.

Throughout Harlem there were many individuals and

situations that served as examples of what not to do. As I

observed the pitfalls others had fallen into, I was able to know

exactly what to do so I could avoid the same snares. In addition,

I always remained humble, never adopting the attitude of, "it

can't happen to me."

Over the years, I absorbed many subtleties of my

environment. One of these subtleties was—despite many of the

buildings in Harlem being dilapidated, the landlords still

maintained ownership. I would sometimes witness the landlord,

or their representative, coming to place eviction letters on

tenants' doors. I witnessed this occur enough to make me realize

that what seemed like such a stressful occupation to an observer

must have a tremendous upside for them to remain in this

business. There were many wanna be financial advisors surrounding me, yet I kept my observances of landlords in mind as I contemplated how to invest the money I had been saving.

My older co-workers advised me to invest in a 401K plan. Their advice was well received, however once I conducted research about 401k plans, I realized I would not be allowed to access my money until I reached fifty-nine years old. I immediately understood this was not the path for me. I was only twenty-four years old at the time. I viewed the thirty-five year length of time to access my money as a financial jail sentence. I remember thinking if I cannot get rich in thirty-five years with the intellect God had granted me, then something must be wrong with me. As a result, I would hear their financial advice daily and would silently reject it just as often.

As I continued to earn a huge salary and have very few living expenses due remaining in the projects, the money in my savings account accumulated even faster. It became increasingly difficult to hold on to the savings I had amassed. I became increasingly eager to buy a Cuban link chain and Rolex watch. I had heard many great things about real estate as an investment and loved to play Monopoly as a kid. Real estate was booming across the country and television was packed with shows displaying how much wealth can be accumulated from even just one real estate deal.

As the pressure continued to mount however, I considered ignoring my gut instinct and investing in a 401k. After all, it was the safe thing everyone else at my job was doing. The night before going to meet with my employer's benefits department, I sat thinking to myself, "Did doing what everyone else does help me escape the Trap?"

My answer was a resounding no.

These thoughts caused me to reschedule the appointment for a month later. As the days went by, I sat patiently while seeking some form of financial guidance to present itself. One day as I entered my room in my project apartment, for some odd reason I decided to pick up a book I had bypassed hundreds of times before.

This book was purchased by my sister and had collected a good amount of dust over the years. However, this particular day, I gravitated towards it. Maybe it was the title that caught my eye—*Rich Dad, Poor Dad.*

Now that I was somewhat financially mature, I wanted to be a "Rich Dad" one day. Yet another candle had been illuminated in my brain. All the guidance presented by author Robert Kiyosaki seemed as solid as concrete. Perhaps the most influential aspect was the advice about how to retire well before the age of sixty-five through real estate investments.

A few months later, at 25 years young, I purchased my first home in the suburbs of Atlanta, GA for $180,000 by putting a down payment of $36,000 and financing the remaining balance. This home had four bedrooms, three bathrooms, and three thousand square feet sitting on half an acre of land.

Coming from the projects in New York City, this was the biggest house I had ever been in. In fact, my girlfriend, my sister, and I spent a week in the house in the middle of July which can be the warmest part of a Georgia summer. I took pride in watering the lawn the first two days; however, the blazing sun became too much for me to handle. My sister was better equipped due to her military background and therefore I handed the landscaping over to her.

The size of the home was overwhelming as well. I had grown accustomed to tiny two and three-bedroom New York City apartments. The realization that a three thousand square foot house was too much space for two people caused me to revert to my roots and purchase a two-bedroom condo in the Buckhead section of Atlanta and convert the large home into my first rental property.

I was now closer to acquiring the 40 acres my ancestors were promised but never received after slavery ended.

For most of my time in the Trap, I would often hear that "ki's and bricks" were the golden ticket out. These dreams of having "ki's and bricks" of cocaine caused so many of my peers' lives to turn into nightmares.

The *keys and bricks* I now owned were having the opposite effect. They were turning my dreams into reality. The income generated from my first rental property paid for my second vacation out of the United States to the white sand beaches of St. Thomas.

In a matter of four years I acquired six additional rental properties, purchased an Audi and that Range Rover I always spoke about as a kid. I vacationed on numerous islands in the Caribbean.

Our miseducation caused me and so many of my peers to block out the destruction caused by the "ki's and bricks" of cocaine which we so dearly admired. My re-education allowed me to realize the kind of *keys and bricks* I owned through real estate actually opened doors rather than slamming them for life and built foundations for the community instead of destroying them. I now had the REAL keys and bricks that would continue to make a lasting difference in my life as well as others.

As I gained more experience and acquired additional rental properties, I became aware that many of my tenants were working class African American single mothers. Because of my work and wise investing, I now held the power to assist them to further their prosperity. Since I purchased most of these properties far below market value, I had the luxury of not charging the top market rate for rent. This aided these mothers in moving into a home they otherwise could not afford. I took pride in the fact I was often able to delay evictions by allowing some of my tenants to catch up on back rent. I was mindful of the fact evicting them for merely one month's rent was against their interest as well as mine.

Rather than selling drugs to a single mom, I was indirectly supplying hope and perhaps changing the trajectory of two or three generations. Coming from the Trap made me cognizant of the value of a peaceful home in which to study and do homework. This was potentially the difference between a child becoming whatever he or she dreamed of and the child becoming what they were essentially forced to be.

This peaceful environment was the true treasure present in many of the prosperous communities where other races resided. I later learned the quote, "You can't have prosperity without peace." My environment miseducated me to believe the opposite—you cannot have peace without prosperity.

A byproduct of this miseducation led me to believe all Caucasians were rich and only had peace because of this. I accepted this ideology for a while, until I looked at the immigrant communities of the upper west side in which many of my childhood classmates lived. My curiosity led me to look at the Chinese and Indian communities throughout New York City. My friends and I would often venture to Chinatown to steal, or as we called it "racking" (short for racking up).

In the midst of "racking" I would observe the neighborhoods and quickly noticed the

Chinese people were not dressed in designer clothes and their

buildings were not fancy either. So, in many ways their

circumstances were similar to ours. The main difference was

their neighborhoods had much less violence. As I continued to

study the disparities between neighborhoods, I was fortunate to

have an aunt who had a small house in South Ozone Park,

Queens. The house was modest, but it was by far better than any

housing project apartment.

The neighborhood was comprised of mostly West Indian and

Indian families. I would visit every summer and would be in awe

of how peaceful it was and the fact I rarely saw a police car. My

aunt worked as a housekeeper and had three kids, all of whom

attended a nearby private school. I would often ask myself how

my life would be if I lived with her. One great difference would

have been my educational experience. I would not have dealt

with going through metal detectors or being on defense every day on the train ride home from school. I would have had the treasure of peace I was missing in the Trap.

When I would return to my projects, I would imagine what it would be like to be able to study without the stress of the sounds of sirens blaring and thirty dudes standing outside of my building.

I once encountered a Caucasian patient at the hospital where I worked. She appeared to be in her twenties and explained to me she lived in the Battery Park section of Manhattan. I immediately had two thoughts— "man her parents must be rich" and "I wish I lived in Battery Park."

I complimented her on living in such a nice area. She debunked my prejudicial thoughts by quickly letting me know her rent was approximately $5000 per month and was being split amongst five roommates in a two-bedroom apartment. I asked her, "why would you share such a small apartment with so many people?" She replied, "because it's so quiet and peaceful down there."

She went on to further explain her roommates worked opposite shifts as bartenders and waitresses in order to accommodate their living conditions. The combination of all these nuances helped me understand that all Caucasians were not rich financially, however a great majority were privileged to live in a peaceful environment. It appeared to me their entire existence was rooted in this fact.

I continued observing the dynamics of society, I learned many of the areas where the best beaches and parks are located throughout America seemed to be inhabited mostly by Caucasians and other races besides African- Americans. Naturally, the more peaceful your environment, the clearer your mind would become and therefore the easier it would be to achieve the grades needed to be accepted into a top college and become a highly paid professional such as a doctor or lawyer.

I wondered if this perhaps was the reason there were so many doctors and lawyers from backgrounds different than mine and perhaps in a different environment would I have been a doctor instead of a radiology tech.

Yet another example of my miseducation was the way I viewed people who had been shot. Growing up in Harlem during the late 1980's and 1990's caused me to have admiration for anyone who survived being shot. I mistakenly viewed these individuals as bulletproof superheroes. However, later in life working in trauma hospitals provided even more material towards my overall re-education.

I began to take inventory of the racial make-up of the victims of violence compared to the racial make-up of those responsible for their healthcare. It was ironic to me that it was extremely unbalanced. 95 % of the victims of violence were Black or Hispanic, while 85% of the doctors were Caucasian. If this were a Libra scale it would certainly even out, however the reality was the scales of society were imbalanced.

A typical victim of a gunshot to the chest or abdomen could possibly provide training for at least six different types of doctors. Upon the victim's arrival, they would typically be treated initially by an emergency room doctor and trauma surgeon. Once the patient is stabilized, they would most likely have treatment from a pulmonologist, gastroenterologist, radiologist if an infection occurs, and pathologist who interprets the specimen collected by the radiologist.

Although this training is desperately needed by these doctors, upon hearing the stories of these gunshot victims, the senselessness began to wear on my conscious. I would often wish the much needed experience the doctors were gaining could be acquired from fewer Black and Hispanic victims.

While other communities were producing doctors like a factory, my community was producing prisoners and gunshot victims at an even greater rate. A great majority of these victims were shot for ridiculous reasons. I have spoken to gunshot victims who were shot during an attempted robbery when they had nothing of value in their possession, but they were still shot anyway. On the opposite end of the spectrum, I have spoken to robbers who became victims by trying to rob someone who had no money on them but did possess a firearm and turned the tables on them. I always questioned why people continue to attempt to rob someone without knowing if the person actually has anything of value on them. Perhaps because in the trap, many of us seek to acquire a reputation as a so called "stick up kid".

I vividly remember a nineteen-year-old who was shot right between the eyes for attempting to burglarize a home. According to the police officer who was guarding him, this young man failed to kick the front door down three times, but on the fourth attempt he was successful. Unfortunately for him the homeowner waiting on the other side with a .44 Magnum. This incident was particularly sad due to the double dose of consequences he had to face for his actions by being forever maimed and possibly forever incarcerated.

Getting shot or being a robber has been continuously glorified for far too long in urban environments and entertainment. Perhaps one day these same individuals who could have possibly been gunshot victims become our future lawyers and doctors.

Probably the most outrageous piece of miseducation I received in the Trap was that entertainment and sports were the only ways for us to succeed legally in life. Even as a kid when I would hear Hip Hop artist say this repeatedly, it would irritate me because I knew it was a lie. They would often state, "You better be happy we are making music, otherwise we would be robbing your ass right now."

This never made sense to me because I knew there were other ways of escaping the Trap. I never really heard of many musicians born into the Trap elevate to living on Park Avenue;

however, the lawyer my mom worked for as a caretaker certainly did.

There is a saying, "I'd rather have ten lions than one hundred sheep." Well, I would rather have one hundred lawyers and doctors emerge from my neighborhood than one athlete or entertainer. Perhaps this motto was because I had a different point of reference than many others in trap due to seeing the African American lawyer my mom worked for daily. This myth caused so many of us to not even attempt anything else. Once we saw the dream of becoming an entertainer or athlete slipping away, we often decided to give up on achieving success. I can remember my friend saying if he does not get "on" by twenty-five years old he was going to pursue a rap career. There was one problem, he was not pursuing any other avenues to reach his dreams. Therefore, he should have just began honing his skills as a rapper long before the age of twenty-five. Like so many of us, he appeared to be hoping for winning a lawsuit or the lottery as a means to escaping the Trap. Even with all of my optimism and the positive images I had been exposed to, I too felt if I wasn't

"on" by twenty-five then I would pursue music or drug dealing to

the best of my abilities.

Navigating our way out of the Trap permanently was difficult to

do even temporarily. So many of us were overly loyal to our

neighborhoods. Our mothers, fathers, grandparents, and even

some great grandparents grew up here. In my case, I was a first-

generation project baby. I believe this is what allowed me to

have less of an emotional attachment to my neighborhood. My

lack of emotions tied to the community allowed me to be curious

and frequently venture out. I can always remember having a

burning desire to explore what was going on in other areas of

New York City. I would purposely pursue girlfriends who lived in

Brooklyn and Queens due to wanting to experience what it was

like to live in a house rather than an apartment. Often when

headed to these areas after hanging out on my block, my friends

would call me crazy for going out of "district." This was similar to

what I learned in school where many black people were made to feel uncomfortable when traveling even a few blocks east or

west into other districts throughout the Jim Crow era in the U.S.

and Apartheid in South Africa. This mentality was such a contrast

to that of so called "white" people. In studying the history of

Caucasian people, they seemed to explore and even conquer

whatever area they deemed fit. In fact, the exploration of the

world by Europeans is what has granted them the privilege and

power they have today.

I quickly realized the ability to roam around freely is

what partly made one a whole human being. This exploration

did not only relate to history, it was relevant to current events

in my life.

In Harlem during the early 2000's there became a gradual

increase of Caucasians moving into the area. This trend was

unique to me since I had never once seen a large portion of

African Americans gradually moving into Caucasian

neighborhoods. I wondered why Caucasians would want to move

into the Trap which so many of us were so loyal to. We as African

Americans certainly did not seem to have the same freedom or resources to move out of the Trap into Caucasian neighborhoods in the same large numbers.

As the numbers of Caucasians in Harlem continued to grow, the previous names of the area's largest sections slowly began to be altered. I first witnessed this trend as I watched a news report related to the area my brother's housing project was located. All the previous news reports I had ever heard about this area were referred to simply as "Harlem." I was perplexed to hear the news reporter say, **"reporting live from Morningside Heights."**

Did they rezone or redistrict this area or was the reporter somehow mistaken? This new name definitely served to create a new benevolent mental image of the neighborhood in my mind as well others and it certainly worked.

This methodology was a stark contrast to the miseducation inserted in me throughout my childhood in which those of us in the Trap glorified the malevolent aspects of our

neighborhoods and actually gave them negative names.

One example of this was the Drew Hamilton Housing

project I grew up in. In order to make the neighborhood seem

more menacing we began referring to it as ZOO HAMILTON.

Yes!!! We, as African American human beings who hated for

racists to refer to us as animals such as monkeys and gorillas,

were now saying we live in a **ZOO.** A resident of Drew Hamilton

projects did actually have a full-grown tiger living in his

apartment for years before it was discovered by the New York

City Police Department. This nickname served to keep us on the

same notorious footing as the other neighborhoods like Brooklyn

which was being called "Brooknam" (Vietnam), or "Murderville"

(Manhattanville Projects), Killadelphia (Philadelphia), and so on.

Just as a good name can allow for a neighborhood to

thrive, adopting a negative name will not allow for such. In fact,

these names planted more seeds which caused an increased

appetite for making the neighborhood more notorious. It was a twisted ideology in which there was a perverted value in the

neighborhoods' increased crime rate. However, when the

Caucasians moved in to gentrify the exact same neighborhoods,

the occupants seemed to rapidly lose the desire for increasing

the neighborhoods' notoriety. It was as if white angels flew in to

make the neighborhood gentler, hence the term gentrify.

Over time, these neighborhoods did in fact become

gentler. Caucasian females could run in booty shorts AT NIGHT

without being harassed even though African American women

have been verbally disrespected for years while walking past

these same blocks with not an inch of skin showing. I can

remember multiple incidents where a female rejected the

advances of guys I used to hang on the block with and

consequently glass bottles were thrown at them. Every time I

witnessed this, the ignorance of it all never sat well with me. I

always wondered why I never saw other communities

disrespecting their woman so blatantly. One of my biggest fears

throughout my adolescence was someone in my neighborhood

disrespecting a female member of my family thereby leading me

to retaliate with violence and receiving a prison sentence.

A gentler neighborhood is certainly a positive thing if the

gentleness trickles down to the pre-existing residents. As this

gentrification occurred, it became my hope that the same

reverence granted to the new residents would be equally

distributed to the natives. The gentrification of Harlem began to

cause native Harlemites to question how it was possible they did

not see the potential of such a culturally rich area. Near the area

of a hole in the sidewalk I planned to jump in for a lawsuit in

hopes of escaping the trap, for years there were abandoned

brownstones which were once crack houses. Bradhurst and

Edgecombe Avenues were previously notorious drug blocks. As

the gentrification increased, a rumor began to swirl that for

decades the city had previously offered these same properties

for sale for one dollar. Admittedly, these properties were

dilapidated, and their potential was perhaps difficult to see, but

if the natives would have banded together to acquire them it could have caused a positive domino effect to occur throughout

Harlem.

It's easy to have an idealistic point of view from my

current position in life, however when living day to day under the

stresses of the Trap, investing for twenty years down the line is

understandably the last thing on one's mind.

From as young as I can remember most residents of the

Trap were either stagnant, living day to day, or living fast. Most

of us between the ages of sixteen and twenty-five were living

fast lives. Even if we were not living fast lives in a traditional

sense by committing crimes, we were living fast in our minds by

wanting to be grown beyond our chronological ages. We viewed

ourselves as grown men who should have all the luxuries of life

before the age of twenty-five. This mentality created a false

sense of urgency which led so many of us right into a

trap.

I can recall leaving the projects to attend college in Atlanta. Unfortunately, I was forced to return two and a half years later after finishing. I was a mere twenty years old and already considered myself a failure while other kids in the suburbs were afforded their entire twenties to achieve so called success. Due to my embarrassment I began avoiding everyone in my neighborhood upon my return because of my perceived failure. The stress and pressure I felt was slowly leading me to consider taking desperate measures to achieve success and escape the Trap. A couple of my friends were bringing in steady income from their street endeavors therefore the allure was intense. I recall a conversation in front of my project building with a close friend who bought the first model Yukon Denali released in 2003. As we conversed, I looked up at my twenty-one-floor high building and said, "*I don't know if I'm ever going to make it out of here.*" He replied, "*nah take your time, you are on your way.*"

In a subliminal way, me looking up at my building symbolized my feelings of how daunting the climb would be in order to escape the Trap. Around this time, I sat in my mom's apartment for a whole year only venturing out when necessary. This period was pivotal. It was literally "excel or jail" for so many of us born into the Trap. There was no room for error. I falsely believed the clock of success was rapidly running out at a mere twenty-two years young. My oldest sister was key in counteracting this other piece of miseducation I learned over the years. While I was stagnant, lamenting for months in my mom's apartment with no direction, she suggested that I simply get moving by taking classes and accumulating credits. Her basis was at least I would be further ahead once I decided what direction I would take. This key piece of education would change my life forever, saving me from a life stuck in the Trap.

<u>Hip Hop Road Map</u>

As I continued to assess my plans for escaping the Trap, I realized hip hop and rap music were providing me with a perfect road map. The first song I can remember leading me out of the maze was Slick Rick's *Hey 'Young World.*

This song came out when I was eight years old. Since I did not listen to the radio at all during my earlier years, my first exposure to **Hey Young World** was through seeing the music video. The visual was dramatic and penetrated my soul. The words Slick Rick spoke resonated deeply and were like sunlight beaming into a dark tunnel.

I sat up and paid attention when Slick Rick rapped about the foolishness of dropping out of school. My eyes were opened as he shed light on the fact that hustlers are not people we should admire—they won't be around for long.

My favorite lyric from this song is—

"Don't be a fool like those that don't go to school

Get ahead... and accomplish things

You'll see the wonder and the joy life brings

Don't admire thieves, they don't admire you, their time is limited hard rocks too"

I immediately translated these lyrics into simply— do the right thing and you will likely escape your current situation, while all the robbers and drug dealers who are viewed as hard rocks will most likely be stuck in the Trap for the rest of their lives. It brought full circle for me why many of the hustlers and so-called symbols of success in my neighborhood never actually elevated to a better standard of living. I assessed that it was all an illusion.

Even at such a young age, I could already see through the illusion. The hustlers and robbers in my neighborhood were admired for their big bankrolls, flashy cars, and the respect (fear) they received from others. Hoping to be rich and admired one day too, many children in my neighborhood grew up with hustling as their *career* goal. Fortunately, I was exposed to life outside of my neighborhood, and I saw that hustling was not the only way to get rich. I saw men and women who grew their wealth through education, investments, and businesses. Because I had this expanded perspective, I knew Slick Rick was *dropping jewels*—educating me through facts.

The timing of *Hey Young World* being released was perfect because it served as a foundation for how I was going to navigate my way through the Trap. Armed with the many jewels I absorbed from the song, I ventured out into the neighborhood and began to confirm whether Slick Rick was telling the truth. The most obvious things I noticed were the crack heads, better known as drug addicts, outside of urban America. Many appeared to be longtime drug addicts whose lives had been snatched away, never to return as they once knew it. This was the first example of what I didn't want to become when I got older. I could easily comprehend this wasn't the kind of life I wanted to live. So, at a minimum, even if I never made anything of myself—I was determined NEVER to become a crack head.

It may seem to be a low standard to start with; however, the importance of making this my initial mantra was tremendous. I was merely trying to figure out what I did and didn't want to be, or in a sense what direction I did and didn't want to go.

As I became more familiar with my neighborhood, yet another song resonated with me. Stop the Violence Movement's **Self-Destruction** was released in 1989 when I was nine years old. I'd spent the previous year and a half absorbing the ins and outs of my neighborhood. I realized that certain things which were everyday occurrences in my neighborhood didn't merely boil down to making a choice. Some were ingrained in the fabric of the community. Hearing gunshots at night, bullet holes in the windows and human shit in the staircases were things I had zero control over It was depressing to feel so helpless. However, I slowly accepted my reality.

I decided to focus strictly on my family and me to lessen these feelings of helplessness. In the song *Self-Destruction,* there are many gems that are still relevant today. The constant gunfire and dilapidated living conditions brought on feelings of fear, however when I heard Kool Moe Dee rap—

**"Back in the sixties our brothers
and sisters were hanged, how *could you*
gang bang?
I never ever had to run from the Ku Klux Klan
And I shouldn't have to run from a black man
*Because that's Self Destruction"***

He was talking about the harsh irony of black people being afraid of and killing each other. It is despicable that after having been lynched and tormented by white supremacists like the Ku Klux Klan, we now turn against each other—that's self-destruction.

Kool Moe Dee's words had a triple meaning for me: it made me feel a sense of guilt if I were to ever kill a black man for some silly reason; it gave me a sense of wanting unity; it

empowered me to control my own destiny.

The all-star lineup of rappers featured in *Self-Destruction*

did a great job of highlighting the ills of the ghetto and possible

solutions to these problems.

My second favorite verse is from rapper D-Nice where he
states—

*"It's time to stand together in unity, cause
if not then we're soon to be Self-destroyed,
unemployed, our race will be lost without a
trace"*

He continues—

*"Down the road that we call eternity,
where knowledge is formed, and you'll learn to
be Self-sufficient, independent, to teach to each is
what rap intended, but society wants to invade,
so do not walk this path they laid".*

Growing up in the ghetto, you quickly become fully aware

of the many dark paths you could be led down. Yes, there are

too many to count. As the saying goes, "six million ways to die, choose one." Since statistics in the ghetto are usually double that of the rest of society, you grow up feeling as if there are twelve million ways to die in the hood.

D-Nice made me determined to take careful steps to make certain I was headed down the *path of my own choosing* rather than the path society has laid for us born into the Trap.

I connected the burned-out buildings and terrible living conditions to D-Nice's warning— we would remain destroyed and unemployed if we don't come together as a people.

Indeed, my neighborhood was destroyed, highly unemployed, and consisted of many "lost" individuals. There was a common saying in the ghetto during the late 1980s and early 1990s— "you better sell rock or have a wicked jump shot."

I would often question whether or not I only had two options to improve my reality. Some days I would reject that so-called fact, but most days I accepted it to be true. This all

changed when I heard D-Nice say, ***"where knowledge is formed,***
and you learn to be self-sufficient, independent."

I didn't want to sell drugs, and although I was pretty skilled at basketball, I was not an NBA prospect. D-Nice said I had another option, but I had no idea how actually to make it happen.

I remembered his advice vividly to become independent and self-sufficient by gaining more knowledge, but all I could think was— "Really?! Did D-Nice just tell me that if I gained knowledge, I could become self-sufficient and independent? You mean I have more choices to make it out of here than selling crack rock or shooting a jump shot?!" Now the candle within me had been lit, I already knew the attorney my mom worked for who resided on Park Avenue didn't shoot any jump shots or sell crack rock, but now D-Nice reinforced it while sporting a flat-top haircut, a long leather coat dragging on the floor, with all the swagger I wished to possess one day. I was able to merge these two facts and reject the notion there were only two ways for me and my family to escape the Trap.

Before this epiphany, I probably subconsciously viewed the successful attorney as some superhero who was extraordinary enough to beat the odds. D-Nice allowed me to believe we all can do it without being superheroes.

Around the summer of 1990, my older brother took me under his wing and began to bring me outside with him. We would mostly roll around different areas in Harlem, but sometimes the Bronx as well. At the time, my brother was about seventeen- or eighteen-years-old working at Yankee Stadium. He was making a fairly good living, especially from tips. I admired his tenacity for working and how successful he was for his age without participating in illegal activity. When he wasn't selling beer at Yankee Stadium during baseball season, he was playing neighborhood tackle football without any protective gear. During this time, he was dating an R&B singer whose group debuted a music video on national TV and seemed to be on the brink of

stardom. Needless to say, things were going good for an

eighteen-year old who a couple of years prior only owned three

pairs of pants.

As my brother was riding high, a string of lousy luck

threatened to bring it to a screeching halt. While playing tackle

football that winter in the Bronx's Van Courtland Park, my

brother dislocated his shoulder. Yankee Stadium provided no

health insurance at the time, and my brother was temporarily

forced out of his lucrative gig. Since he had grown accustomed

to this lifestyle, the pressure began to mount. I remember him

waiting for another opportunity to present itself. A few months

passed by and opportunity had yet to come knocking. He

questioned himself daily, asking,

"what the fuck am I supposed to do?"

As he debated with himself and tried to remain patient,

an opportunity finally presented itself, it came in the form of a street entrepreneur offering him a gig. Returning to the days where he had a rotation of three pairs of pants was not in the cards. So, my brother saw the neighborhood drug dealers' offer as one he couldn't refuse. This was my first hands-on experience dealing with the financial pressures of living in the Trap. I initially wondered why my brother didn't merely ask my dad for money when he needed it, I soon realized that once you take on the persona of a fully-grown man, it becomes hard to turn back. The lust for material things can be hard to resist.

Ironically, music was once again aligning with current situations surrounding my life. Sitting at home one day, I was watching a 'popular music video show when a KRS-ONE's video for ***Love's Gonna Get Cha*** was on the television. This video served as a warning about how the need for material things can *getcha* in bad predicaments. The song was eerily similar to the crossroads my brother was currently at in his life. The words KRS-

ONE spoke were like gospel. He rapped—

> *" The very next day while I'm off to class, my mom goes to work cold busting her ass, my sisters cute but has no gear, I got three pair of pants with my brother I share, see when in school I'm made a fool, with 1 ½ pair of pants you ain't cool, but there's no dollars for nothing else, I got beans rice and bread on my shelf, every day I see my mother struggling, now it's time I've got to do something"*.

KRS-ONE highlighted the everyday struggles of life in the ghetto—parents who worked hard but could barely afford to clothe and feed their children. Many of us knew about only having three pairs of pants.

What the fuck am I supposed to do?

My brother, KRS-ONE, and countless others who are born in the Trap are faced with this question numerous times throughout our lives.

As I'm sitting in front of the TV mesmerized by the knowledge KRS-ONE is kicking, he goes even deeper—

*"Here comes Rob and his gold is shimmery, he
gives me $200 for a quick delivery, I do it once, I
do it twice, now there's steak with the beans and
rice, my mother's nervous but she knows the
deal, my sisters gear now has sex appeal, my
family's happy and everything is new, now tell
me what the fuck was I supposed to do?"*

He continues to explain how so many get caught up

dealing drugs. When you're at the end of your rope, and down

to your last dime, a local dealer gives you a few hundred bucks to

make a delivery. It's quick and easy money, so you do it

again...and again...and again. Soon, you have all the money you

want. You can buy new clothes and take care of your family.

Everyone knows what you're doing, but they are caught up too—

they don't like the trouble you could get into, but they don't

want to give up the nice living you are providing.

My brother appeared to be doing very well for himself. I

remember when he bought me my first pair of dressy shoes. I

wore them for two weeks straight, even when playing sports. He treated himself as well—he wore gold jewelry, Sergio Tacchini

sweat suits which were popular amongst the hustlers during this

era, and even had a couple of shearling leather jackets. He

treated me and my sister to a fancy restaurant on the upper east

side of Manhattan. From my perspective, he was doing

something illegal but didn't see him as doing something wrong. I

even served as a lookout as he hustled on 121st street between

7th and 8th avenue. Like KRS –ONE said–as long as his family was

happy, things were okay. Honestly, I hoped he would buy me all

the Air Jordan's I ever wanted.

The thought of my brother ever being incarcerated barely

crossed my mind. He was my brother, my hero, and was way too

clever to be caught, right?

This was the mindset many born into the Trap have.

Either I will get out once I make enough money, I am too smart

to be caught, or if I ever do get caught, I can handle doing a little

jail time. Neither of these three prospects usually materialized, a drug dealer's career often ended with violence or a longer than expected jail sentence due to the heavy-handed drug laws passed during the 1980s.

I was taught in life; there is always a warning before the storm arrives. My brother's warning came while selling crack on a street corner in upper Manhattan. While making his sales, someone was firing off a gun from the roof of a high-rise housing project building. This caused the police to swarm the building immediately. Just as my brother attempted to slip away from all the chaos, a police Sergeant grabbed him by the collar and instead of asking, "where are the drugs?" he asked him, "did you hear where the gunshots are coming from?"

Holding a pocket full of drugs which would have landed him a mandatory five-year prison term, he answered with a considerable crackle in his voice, "Nah, *I haven't heard any gunshots, Officer.*"

Perhaps through divine intervention, this officer was more concerned with the gunshots than making a drug arrest at that moment. For months after that, he struggled with the question of whether he should quit hustling. Was this a sign he needed to quit or just a scare that comes with the territory? After careful consideration, he realized the magnitude of receiving a second chance at life and soon retired from the narcotics business. He began to focus on other means of generating income. The biggest lesson he learned during his time as a drug dealer was that he had the intelligence and business savvy to run his own legal business. He also realized fast money could land you in prison just as fast as you accumulated it. Fortunately for my brother, he survived long enough for his shoulder injury to heal and returned back to working at Yankee stadium within two years. I realized he was basically selling drugs and risking his freedom to buy material items which certainly weren't worth the risk he was taking. His experience of being mere seconds away from incarceration reinforced for me the need to remain legit and never fall to the temptations of growing up in the Trap.

Even though the money was no longer coming in as fast as it once did, his demeanor was that of a much happier man. Rakim rapped on the famous song, *Paid in Full*—

Now I learned to earn because I'm righteous, I feel great, so maybe I might just search for a 9 to 5, and if I strive maybe I'll stay alive.

Knowing that you are earning money the right way not only makes you happier, it keeps you alive longer.

I related the lyrics Rakim spoke to my brother's situation due to the constant images on the evening news of drug dealers being murdered on a regular basis. By this time, my mind had matured to where I could care less about my brother buying me sneakers, I was simply happy he stayed alive through his hustling days.

As my brother began to take a step back from the street life, I became even more comfortable with hanging out on my block and embracing the culture of Harlem. My dad was strictly opposed to me hanging out. He would always say, "Son, there's nothing out there for you."

My mom, on the other hand, seemed to feel I needed to be familiar with my neighborhood and become a stronger young man. Looking back, they both were partially correct.

After digesting all the information, I gathered from my brother's financial crisis, I came to a new-found conclusion— money plays a far more significant role in people's lives than I previously realized. It caused me to adopt a philosophy that made financial stability and staying out of prison the absolute priorities in my life. As I moved around Harlem, I quickly noticed all the guys who were smiling and joking all the time were well put together. Many of the tougher looking guys who were continually frowning were usually the worst dressed. It was easy

for me to decide which side of the equation I needed to be on.

A seed was planted to reinforce my new-found

philosophy when I heard a song by Nas featuring AZ, *Life's a

Bitch*.

It starts off with *AZ* stating—

**" Visualizing the realism of life
and actuality, fuck who's the baddest, a person's
status depends on salary, and my mentality is
money orientated, and I'm destined to live the
dream for all my peeps who never made it".**

Once again, hip-hop lyrics confirmed all the information I

was digesting from the neighborhood daily. Often times being

the toughest or quickest to shoot is incorrectly viewed as the

prized asset in the ghetto. I translated AZ's lyric to mean when

you're older, it won't really matter how much respect you've

gained from violence if you still haven't managed to escape the

Trap.

Nas follows up with—

*" When I was young I used to
do my thing hard, robbing foreigners, take their
wallets, their jewels, and rip their green cards,
then dip to my projects flashing my quick cash,
and got my first piece of ass smoking blunts with
hash, now it's all about cash in abundance,
brothers I used to run with are rich or doing years
in the hundreds, I switched my motto, instead of
saying "fuck tomorrow", that buck that bought a
bottle could've struck the lotto ".*

This was the focal point, where I truly began to live for

my future rather than the next day. I understood Nas wasn't

actually telling me I would win the lottery but was actually telling

me to believe in my future and I just might persevere. I

interpreted the tail end of Nas' verse as doubling down on AZ's

message by basically saying I used to be focused on petty crime,

but now I'm all about financial success-am I going to be

financially successful or doing a hundred years jail time?

This song had some of the most significant influence on

me of any hip song I've heard. It armed me with a philosophy

which made my main priority shift to escaping the Trap

unscathed. It planted seeds of hope, discipline, and patience. No matter what happened along the way, I was now obligated to improve my life and the lives of my family members.

It was now time to begin to make decisions as to which type of brothers *I* was going to *run with*. I began to decide whether I should run with the ballplayers, hustlers, street brawlers, or the rugged, dirty kids who could care less about their future. The choice was rather easy based on the influences of my brother and the hip hop artists whose lyrics resonated with me. I, of course, gravitated towards the ballplayers and well put together brothers in my neighborhood. I was swept into Air Jordan sneaker wave which took America by storm in the late 1980s. I went from being simply happy with my first pair of Air Jordan's to needing a few pairs of high-end Nikes every year. Yes, we were living in the Trap; nonetheless owning just one pair of these shoes provided us with our first feelings of upward mobility. I often wished the Air Jordans could me give the ability to fly my family out of the Trap.

People often question how a pair of sneakers can make one feel empowered. However, living in such a wealth disparaged city like New York, these material goods were the most realistically attainable items we saw. When I rode the train below 96th Street, I would instantly have feelings of inadequacy and defeat come over me.

I would ask myself how my family or I could ever afford to live where movie stars and Wall Street bankers lived.

As I moved from the chain linked fences of the basketball court to hanging out all day and night on the avenue, I began to idolize the "fly guys" of my neighborhood. They were the ones who appeared happiest and were the only African American symbols of success I had seen in person besides the ultra-successful attorney my mom worked for. These guys walked with a confident swagger, which almost made you forget we were living in substandard conditions. They represented hope, and in the ghetto, hope is a priceless commodity.

When I initially started becoming familiar with my neighborhood, I was befriended by two kids who lived on one of the rougher blocks in my area. They lived in buildings known as tenements. These were low-rise privately-owned buildings; many of these were partially abandoned or burned out. Most of the older guys on these blocks looked really tough, but I didn't idolize them because they just didn't have that glow. They looked upset all the time, and their attire wasn't up to par with the guys on the Avenue. As I became more enlightened about the true nature of my neighborhood, I gradually pulled away from these two friends, causing jealousy and resentment which would later lead to a confrontation that could have altered the direction of my life.

The Avenue was almost like a stage where all the ghetto stars gathered. Although the guys on the burned-out blocks weren't the best dressed, many were well respected. Often, I would notice the grungy looking guys roughing up the fly guys. In fact, there was a guy who would randomly knock people out who he perceived as weak, there were a few rare individuals who could navigate both personas. Most of us coming of age usually had to differentiate ourselves as one or the other. If you were a grungy dude who was respected, you still faced the ridicule of being poorly dressed; if you were a fly guy and weren't respected at all, you faced the possibility of having your nice garments taken from you. Also, the pretty girls didn't like the grungy guys as much as the fly guys, however, they also wanted and needed to be with someone who was respected. A female who was involved with someone who was feared and respected had a much easier time walking throughout the neighborhood. Everyone knew not to cross the line with ignorant comments, or else there may be consequences.

If you were able to combine being ruthless with a hustler's ambition, the females were yours for the taking.

Respect was the ultimate currency in the ghetto. It may perhaps have more value to some than money. Usually, by the age of fifteen, we were all aware of this ideology. Therefore, you gradually witnessed your once mild-mannered friends now taking on an extremely more aggressive demeanor. The kid who once had to be in the house before dark, now transformed into a weed smoking stick up kid within a few months. I too was faced with this dilemma because I wanted to be known throughout my neighborhood for *something*-- I just wasn't sure for what exactly.

Residing in the Trap makes you feel like a part of the forgotten many of society. This can cause you to seek the smallest form of recognition from any segment of society, no matter positive or negative. If I'm invisible to the rest of the world, at least my name will be known within a twenty or thirty block radius. This ideology became vivid for me one winter night while a bunch of us neighborhood guys were hanging out on the Avenue. A young African American man was walking past our housing project, talking on a cell phone at a time when having a cell phone was reserved for doctors and drug dealers. One of the older, tougher guys in our crew dared us to rob this individual for his cell phone. In my mind's eye, it didn't make sense to act on his dare because it seemed to come from a place of jealousy. The aspirational mentality ingrained in me made the possibility of me acting on this dare impossible. I remember thinking, "even if he is a drug dealer, he earned that cell phone just like we could if we put our minds to it." I also was concerned that he would come back and retaliate since he probably realized we all hung out in front of this same building every day. The pressure began to mount as the older guy in our crew continued to persuade someone to relieve the kid of his cell phone. He said, "What, y'all scared or something? Y'all ain't no wolves."

They say *pressure busts pipes*, and in this case, it proved true. One of the guys I least expected to succumb to the pressure actually did. He seemed to comprehend that if he were successful at robbing the kid for his cell phone, his reputation would instantly grow larger. So, he decided to confront the kid and take the cell phone.

At first, even I was slightly in awe at what he had just done, but then I thought of two distinct rap songs that addressed these kinds of situations. His reputation indeed instantly grew larger. The whole neighborhood spoke about this particular incident for about a week straight.

Legendary rap group, Gangstarr, had a great song called **Just to Get a Rep** which spoke of a neighborhood stick up kid who gained notoriety from his numerous felonious capers. Guru, one half of the group, Gangstarr, rapped, **"brothers are amused by other brothers' reps.'**

He continues—

**Some might say he's a
dummy, but he's sticking you and taking all your
money--it's a daily operation; a lot of brothers
know his name-so he thinks he's got a little bit of
fame from the stick-up game.**

The rep grows bigger, now he's known for his trigger finger, he's at the peak of his crazy career... but as we all know the things we do come back and he's not seeing peeps are scheming to counteract...his time ran out, his number came up, and that's it-some brothers gotta go out just to get a rep.

These lyrics informed me it was illogical to commit crimes against people in your very own neighborhood since they would easily be capable of retaliation or easily be able to point you out to law enforcement. In a sense it was a form of cannibalism. The probabilities of you ending up dead or in jail from committing crimes against your own community were extremely high. In this case, the guy from my neighborhood was arrested about a month after he committed the robbery. This was right around the time all the hoopla had died down from the incident. I believe he received a ten-year sentence for robbery and assault. By the time he was released from prison, cell phones were no longer an exclusive item. In fact, almost everyone had one.

Could you imagine doing ten years in prison for stealing an item which a few years later was being given out basically for free?

That would have to be a hard pill to swallow.

There are countless examples of identical situations where young African American men have destroyed their lives while gaining no reward from the crime committed. Many of these individuals were once great students with great hearts, who due to the negative pressures of the Trap deemed it necessary to take on a persona contrary to who they were really meant to be.

Nas; song **The Message**, has a line at the end of the first verse which speaks to this often-sudden transformation—

"Yo, overnight thugs' bug
because they ain't promised shit, hungry ass-
hooligans stay on that piranha shit."

Just as a piranha will eat anything if it's hungry without considering the repercussions, a deprived young person with little hope for the future will do whatever is necessary to fill the void created by being born into the Trap. The irony is, the allure of "hood fame" can actually hypnotize an individual into believing his name is not just ringing bells within a thirty-block radius, he believes he is actually a somebody to the mainstream world. The sad reality is he remains an invisible man to the greater society. Once he acquires a criminal record, he will be essentially deleted from mainstream society as easily I can delete the words I'm typing on this page. Once you have assisted society in deleting you, the only option becomes living a life of doing what you *have to do* instead of a life doing things you *want to do*.

As I grew through adolescence, more and more of my peers were being "deleted" from society. A majority of the deletions were due to robbery and drug dealing. I would often feel as if there was literally someone sitting behind a giant computer pressing a delete button every time one of my friends was incarcerated. I realized with the way society operates, a criminal record basically turned you into the walking dead.

It was almost as if the African American community was part of a social experiment to see how many of us could escape the conditions we were living under. Sort of a sick high stakes science project which we had to figure out. For me, being deleted from society wasn't an option, the stakes were simply too high.

De La Soul, a popular rap group during the late 1980s and early 1990s, spoke to this on the song "**Stakes Is High**". Group member, Pos, rapped— *"**people go through pain but**

still don't gain."*

I related this to the many men in my neighborhood who were suffering incarceration and had little to nothing to show for the crimes they committed. I never heard stories of money buried away or locked in some secret location. The older

gangsters in my neighborhood used to jokingly say "crime pays"

as a greeting. It was clear, crime doesn't pay as handsomely as

we were led to believe. So then, why were we doing it?

The crystal-clear answer to this question still evades me to this day. Pos also rapped— ***"experiments where needles and skin connect, no wonder where we live is called the projects! When them stakes is high you damn sure try to anything to get a piece of the pie, electrify even die for the cash"***.

After processing this entire song, I would ask myself when

this horrible social experiment was going to end, ***or better yet***

when we as a people were going to force it to end. I realized we

were being conditioned to pursue options that had extremely

long odds while other communities were pursuing options that

had extremely good odds of success. In my community, the only

hope of attaining a better life was becoming a professional

athlete, possibly getting a government job such as a postal

worker or correction officer or becoming a successful criminal.

Yes, you are reading correctly—a successful criminal!

Many of us genuinely believed there was a good chance of becoming successful via criminality. We were allowed to become *street dreamers.* We bought into the fantasy sold to us through various gangster movies we loved to watch repeatedly. The drugs my brother peddled as I served as the lookout were even branded the image from the "Godfather" movie. The level of ridiculousness of our mentality is exemplified in the fact we had seen numerous other young brothers killed and incarcerated. Every hustler I've ever known seemed to think their dream was going to end differently than the hustlers who failed before them.

Nas, a rapper who obviously had a great influence on my life, again aided me in rejecting the lies we are led to believe in the Trap. On his songs, **Street Dreams, (remix featuring R. Kelly), the chorus states—**

Street Dreamer, ooh mercy mercy me, there ain't nothing out there for ya, situations get heavy, heavy when you're tryna be a gangster.

Living under the conditions of the Trap causes not only a heavy, heavy burden on your shoulders but also places a heavy, heavy burden on your heart. I believe R. Kelly repeated the word heavy twice to emphasize the true weight of the burden.

Nas plays his part with a jeweled filled second verse in which he states–

"Black clouds over the hood I'm on the corner with the thugs, late night under the moon as they assume I'm slinging drugs, cause I'm hooded up (wearing a hoodie), thought a G night wasn't good enough (a $1000 a night profit), pushed my luck, then they had a brother put in cuffs, luckily I made it out of court comfortably, judge said I need to get a job, ain't nothing coming free, could've gotten a one to three(1 -3 years in prison), I try to school these shorties under me, but they can't see, so we're back to where we never left, the ghetto it's a damn shame, knowing it's a man's game, shorty I think it's time you make your plans change, all of that running around tryna chase what's already here been there, it's going nowhere".

My second or third time hearing this song was when I experienced a *light bulb* moment which helped me grasp the fact, we were living for a false dream, which would one day turn into a nightmare.

In the ghetto, we were extremely impressionable. It was no wonder we followed whatever was deemed cool at the time. I remember when Spike Lee's movie, *Clockers*, was released. This movie depicted the lives of young black men living in a housing project in Brooklyn, New York. In our eyes, their lives were remarkably similar to ours. The lead character, Strike, played by Mekhi Phifer, developed a love for drinking a chocolate drink to soothe his ulcers. Even though none of us were suffering from ulcers, we began to copy and mimic Strike's behavior by drinking Kahlua Mudslides every day for about two straight weeks. The older guys would buy them for us from the liquor store. We all wanted to be just like Strike until we all began to suffer from diarrhea. Our goal was accomplished; we now had the first-hand experience of what Strike went through in *Clockers*. Ironically, we viewed ourselves as more authentic after this experience, even though we were subconsciously mimicking a movie.

There are countless examples of entertainment, having a heavy influence on the Trap. One glaring example is the nicknames we adopted. Even though there wasn't even one family in the Trap who was Sicilian, Irish, or Colombian, but yet many of the guys in the neighborhood had nicknames such as Luciano, Siegel, Nitty, Capone, Scarface, and Montana. The list goes on and on, but I would say Capone, Nitty, and Scarface were the most used. There could be three or four individuals within a thirty or forty block radius with the different variations of the same nickname. One guy would be nicknamed Al Capone, a second would be called Ty Capone, and a third would be named simply Capone. It was easy to differentiate them based on what they were best known for. It usually worked out where one would be a killer, the other a stick-up artist, and the third a mid to high-level drug dealer.

I wondered if the nicknames came about due to the individual or the individual came about due to taking on the persona of the nickname. I concluded that the individual usually took on the persona of the nickname. Once you had a nickname like Capone, you basically had to personify that title just as a doctor or nurse must personify a medical professional. In essence, you had to be the most felonious Capone, Luciano, or Nitty you could muster.

Even the guns circulating in the neighborhood seemed to mimic the guns we saw and heard of through entertainment. The three most popular guns idolized during my era were the Smith and Wesson, Desert Eagle, and the TEC-9. Simultaneously, everyone who had guns added the Smith and Wesson 9mm handgun to their arsenal.

The second most popular gun was probably the Desert Eagle, or as we called it, *the Desert E*. It sounded a lot more street when we said, "I got the Desert E," or "My man was toting the Desert E." My first time hearing about a Desert Eagle was on the song,

Affirmative Action by the Firm.

Affirmative Action featured AZ, Cormega, Foxy Brown, and Nas. On this Mafioso themed song, Cormega raps—

> ***"When you re-up, bring your***
> ***heater, or your cream goes between us, real shit***
> ***my Desert Eagle got an ill grip".***

Instantly I thought to myself, "the Desert Eagle must be the best gun to have because

Cormega said so and the grip on it must be insanely good."

Being naïve to how big this gun actually was, I figured even if it were too big and I fired it, it would remain in my hand no matter what. I also assumed it was the perfect gun for me since I'd never shot a gun before and having this gun would transform me into an instant marksman if ever need be. It is ironic years later after moving to the south as an adult, I was legally allowed to carry whatever firearm of my choosing due to me not having a felony on my record.

Rounding out the top three was the TEC-9 machine gun. It was like an updated version of the Thompson submachine gun (tommy gun) used by mobsters in the 1930's. The TEC-9 could be held with two hands similar to Sylvester Stallone in the *Rambo* movies which were popular with us also. Seeing Rambo unload his machine gun was alright, but it simply didn't have the same effect on me when compared to Nas speaking about the

TEC-9 he pulled from his dresser. With tremendous frustration in his voice, on the song

Represent, Nas goes" Nas laments--

**"a rebel of the street corner,
pulling a TEC out the dresser, police got me under
pressure."**

The word TEC itself made me feel as though it could give superhero power. When listening to this song even for the first time, you could instantly imagine a TEC-9 was a powerful gun from the inflection in Nas' voice.

One summer, I got into a fist fight and received the only black eye I've ever had in my life. One of my slightly older friends got news of my condition and immediately offered me- you

guessed it - the opportunity to retaliate by shooting up my

enemy's' entire block with a TEC-9. See my point? He could have

offered me any type of gun, but during that era, the TEC was the

gun you wanted to use to send a resounding message.

There were a lot of guns in my neighborhood, but I never

once saw a gun shop in New York City. I would always question

how they got into the neighborhood. The anger I felt during this

time caused me to contemplate my friend's offer seriously. I felt

disrespected just at the fact I had a black eye-it didn't matter

whether it was a fair fight.

Two distinct things prevented me from airing my enemy's

block out during this time. The first deterrent was an incident my

brother described in which he got into an argument with a

female acquaintance. During the disagreement, my brother

proceeded to smack this young lady without considering the

possible repercussions. This incident happened when I was

young, but I remember him describing it so vividly about five years after it occurred. He described how the female's uncle who happened to be a bigtime drug dealer came knocking on his apartment door accompanied by his crew and a few 12-gauge shotguns. My brother wasn't home, but his mom was. She answered the door but didn't open it as is standard protocol in the projects. We were taught to look through the peephole first before ever opening the door. There was also another rule in the projects-don't hurt women and children as they are considered civilians. Through what I believe was another divine intervention for my brother, the individuals who came looking for him left without harming anyone. I am fairly certain, as was he, he would have been killed if he were home.

This story made me once again understand that we were all stuck in a trap which everything we did affect each other. We were all in each other's crossfire. Therefore, it's best we learn how to get along. I couldn't fathom the thought of putting my mom in danger. I'd better swallow my pride since it would be a no-win situation if my family were harmed, and I ended up in prison for retaliating.

I had also witnessed people retaliate after losing a fight, completely miss the intended target, and hit innocent bystanders in the process. All these things caused me to pause before retaliating, but nothing affected my decision not to seek revenge more than 2 Pac's song, *Trapped.*

Many people in my neighborhood expected me to retaliate during the period of tension between my adversary and me. In fact, he even seemed to expect retaliation also. We both appeared to be plotting our next move. One day it was about 90 degrees, and he was wearing a hooded sweatshirt at three o'clock in the afternoon. Ghetto etiquette taught us when someone is wearing a hoodie when it's 90 degrees, it's not because they want to sweat off pounds, but more likely they are holding a firearm. I began to wear my fitted baseball cap low and coming outside only at sundown. I also began consulting people from other neighborhoods who he didn't know, but I did, who

wanted to exact revenge on him for me. We pondered the

method of revenge for about two weeks. Things were about to

get pretty violent, but I understood for every *action* there is a

reaction. 2 Pac's song, *Trapped*, spoke of an altercation which

escalated to gun violence. The words were so prophetic, and if it

weren't for this song, I might literally have been still

incarcerated. *Trapped* actually spared me from being trapped

forever in the prison system.2 Pac rapped so eloquently—

" You know they got me
trapped in this prison of seclusion, happiness,
living on the streets is a delusion, and even a
smooth criminal one day must get caught, shot
up or shot down with the bullet that he bought,
nine millimeter kickin', thinking what the streets
do to me, cause they never talk peace in the black
community, all we know is violence….. Walk the
city streets like a rat pack of tyrants, too many
brothers headed for the big Pen, comin' out
worse off than when they went in."

This portion of the song told me to give peace a chance.

All we know is retaliation and violence, but perhaps I should try a different approach. Giving peace a chance was easier said than done, especially when numerous people are ridiculing you for having a black eye and expecting you to retaliate. The black eye wasn't an easy pill to swallow, however looking back, revenge wouldn't have been worth the cost. The ridicule was intense enough to make you question whether other people were going to force your hand in the future because they now view you as weak. Certainly, in hindsight for the price I could live with my decision.2 Pac helped ease my fears by rapping—

"Now I'm trapped and need to find a getaway, all I need is a "G" ($1000)and somewhere safe to stay, can't use the phone, cause I'm sure someone's tapping in, I did it before, ain't scared to use my gat (gun) again-I look back in hindsight the fight was irrelevant, but now he's the devil's friend, it's too late to be tellin' him, he shot first I'll be damned if I run away, homie is done away, I SHOULD HAVE PUT MY GUN AWAY, I WASN'T THINKING, ALL I HEARD WAS THE RIDICULE, GIRLIE'S LAUGHIN', SAYING DAMN HOMIES DISSIN YOU, I fired my weapon, started steppin' in the hurricane, I got shot, so I dropped feeling a burst of pain…… now I'm a fugitive to be hunted like a murder…..what do I do? Live my life in a prison cell? I rather die

than be trapped in a living hell, they got me trapped".

I could literally hear 2 Pac's voice in my head during the two weeks or so in which I was contemplating revenge. I came to the realization I wouldn't be retaliating for myself, but mostly for the image, I needed to uphold for other people. Having a black eye angered me, but I previously had facial injuries from playing sports. Therefore, I knew my good looks would return in a matter of a week or so.

About two weeks had passed, and I could feel the temperature cool down around the altercation. I could see all the fears I had about being tested in the future were unfounded. Needless to say, time and 2 Pac saved me from overreacting to a fist fight and destroying my life. In a twist of irony, eleven years later, the kid I got into an altercation with was shot in the face and left severely disfigured by someone he got in a fist fight with. The night I got news of him being shot, I remember looking up at the stars and breathing a sigh of relief. I couldn't help but think how angry I would have been at myself learning of this news while serving a long sentence in a cold prison cell. These revelations placed an even greater emphasis on my freedom. It caused me to see how close I came to allow someone to snatch away my freedom. In essence, 2 Pac summed it up for me- *"do I live my life in a prison cell? I'd rather die than be trapped in this living hell."*

Every time I would hear this song or see the video, I internally changed the last part of the lyric from *"they got me trapped"* to *"they'll never have me trapped."*

<u>The Truth Set Me Free</u>

Throughout my years of living in the Trap, I came to realize our most significant obstacles were not the physical barriers around us—our most significant obstacles were the barriers we created in our own minds.

Many false assumptions were placed on us by society, and often, the lack of hope caused us to accept them as fact. I would often see news reports of how terrible my neighborhood was, yet I more often than not saw people conducting themselves in a very morally sound manner, including the most hardened criminals and drug dealers.

When we hung out in the lobbies of our project buildings, we would always be sure to hold doors for ladies as they entered and lower our voices until they got onto the elevator. It was an innate quality the neighborhood instilled in us. We never discussed why or where we learned these morals, they were always done without any hesitation. Perhaps it was because we wanted our moms and grandmas to have the same peace when they entered the building. Whatever the reason, I am glad this unwritten rule was present. Could you imagine your mom coming home from work and you having to escort her in and out of the building every day? That is a duty no one should have forced upon them unless they are training to become a bodyguard, and definitely not a duty a teenager should have to concern himself with. In some other neighborhoods, these unwritten rules were not followed as consistently. I thank God they were adhered to in mine because being a personal bodyguard for all the women in my family would have been one more extraordinary duty added to daily life in the Trap.

We certainly would have been fit for the task of being a bodyguard due to often coming of age incredibly early. Due to our environment, by the time we were fifteen years old, we had many characteristics of grown men, such as critical thinking skills, financial savvy, and strong leadership. By this age, many of us also had numerous unpleasant interactions with police officers, which gradually instilled a soldier like mentality. The good traits instilled in us had a simultaneously unfortunate negative consequence. We actually began to believe we were indeed grown men and began to set unrealistic expectations for ourselves. More affluent areas of allowed children to actually be children, while our environment torpedoed us from boys to men in just a few years of hanging out in the streets. Many of us believed we needed to have a pocket full of money, engage in the most sex with as many as females possible, and be responsible for the financial security of our entire family before reaching puberty. Can you see the irony of a fifteen-year-old assuming the financial burden of his entire family? There are grown men of all races and ethnicities with college degrees who cannot shoulder the burden of taking care of their families on one income, therefore imagine the pressure a boy feels from such a responsibility. He is highly inclined to be easily influenced and misled by anything that remotely appears to have the ability to alleviate him of these pressures. The by-product of these pressures and ensuing mentality caused many of us to follow paths which have been proven time and time again to lead to a life filled with pain and suffering.

The false trail, which perhaps was most widely followed in my neighborhood, was drug dealing. Young boys trying to be men somehow believed selling drugs was the ideal profession and would lead to a better life. The knowledge my brother shared with me about the *game*, coupled with the fact I didn't see anyone truly escaping the Trap by following the drug dealing map, caused me to wonder why more of the older guys who suffered before us didn't try harder to steer us in the right direction.

I often asked myself—was it because this failed mentality was so ingrained in the neighborhood? Had we lost all hope and become resigned to our painful destiny? Or, was it because they missed out on their opportunity for a more peaceful life and did not want the new generation to leave them behind?

I believe it is a combination of all three.

This opinion was formed based on the premise, if I were lured into a trap which caused me to endure endless pain and suffering, would it not be my duty to warn those who were heading towards the same trap which ensnared me? If I did not pass on this information to those coming after me, it would certainly have to be because I didn't realize the true effects of being ensnared. I reasoned, if I refused to share my knowledge with others, it was ultimately because either I had given up and decided there was not a viable way to escape, or I was just really selfish and wanted to see others stuck in the trap with me.

The latter was a clear example of the crabs in the barrel mentality in the trap we so often hear of. There was a saying in Harlem which became the name of a basketball tournament, **Each One Teach One**. However, this mantra never fully took on its profound greatness. This phrase, if fully emphasized by the community, can lead each new generation down the correct path to escaping the trap without all the suffering the elders endured before them.

There was often a feeling when someone managed to *make it out* of the neighborhood that they were *lucky*. After all, we were trained to believe the lie that the only way to get out of the Trap was to have your lucky break in sports or entertainment.

This lie was constantly perpetuated, pushing the idea of *luck* on us hoping we would never realize the truth. If we continued to believe that getting out of the Trap was somehow like *hitting the lottery*, we would wait for our big break instead of putting in the work to get a and strive for more.

I personally rejected this mentality by rationalizing if there are thousands of professions throughout the world, why would we be only limited to a few of them? I initially embraced a defeatist mindset until I realized the equation above was quite illogical. While we believed we were limited to three figurative basketball hoops to try to make a shot in the game of life, for generations the rest of the world was taught to believe, they had an unlimited number of hoops to try and score a basket.

This analogy came to me one cold winter day on the basketball court in my projects. I realized that not only were we shooting at an extremely limited number of basketball hoops compared to the rest of society, but we were also shooting into extremely narrow hoops due to the low odds of becoming successful at the three so-called professions which were supposed to improve our standard of living.

It was like the rigged basketball hoop games at the amusement parks—you are practically guaranteed to lose. This was another eureka moment for me. I decided I would open my mind to the unlimited number of *hoops* life has to offer, and I wanted my *hoops* to be as wide as possible. I was determined— my odds of scoring would be as high as the other races throughout America.

A few years before this eureka moment, I viewed the future as

bleak and my hopes for escaping the Trap very slim. I would

often brainstorm ways to achieve financial success with the least

amount of effort but would come up empty. I would hear stories

of people winning multimillion-dollar lawsuits and escaping the

Trap forever. The more I listened to these stories, the more I

began to focus on winning a lawsuit as the fourth long-shot

possibility of moving my family out of the Trap. One day an

ingenious idea came over me while walking down a hill on 145th

Street, between Bradhurst and 8th Avenue. As my friend and I

were walking, I noticed there was a hole in the sidewalk which

was not covered by any orange cones or surrounded by any

yellow caution tape. I made the instant assumption that if either

of us "*accidentally*" fell into this hole and suffered some non-life-

threatening injuries, we would be able to forever keep our

families out of the hole we were born into by winning a lawsuit.

The hole in the sidewalk was just big enough for an average sized

male to get stuck in and not go plunging into the gates of hell. I waited a few weeks to tell my friend about this idea since I was sure he would want me to be the one to plunge myself into the hole while he played the role of the witness. My cause for concern was validated a few weeks later when I shared my harebrained scheme with him. I expected him to be a lot more receptive to the general idea; however, he quickly dismissed it as a long-shot and downright dangerous. The rejection received from him was surprising since I was certain he was equally, if not more, desperate as I was to find a way out of the Trap. Out of my desperation and hopelessness, I continued to recruit friends who I viewed as brave and clever enough to pull off this scheme with me for about six months without any success. I was disappointed no one would join me because I now realized most of my friends had even less hope of escaping the Trap than I did.

In my opinion, their unwillingness to participate in my harebrained scheme had more to do with an acceptance of life in the Trap than some moral code they were adhering to. I eventually came to see the immorality in receiving a cash settlement from a lawsuit due to a manufactured accident and

began to hear a voice which told me since I was clever enough to

manage the horrors of living in the Trap so well and devise this

clever but illegal scheme, I was certainly capable of navigating

my way out of the Trap legally.

I began to weigh my odds of becoming successful from

sports or entertainment and soon realized that even though I

was a particularly good basketball player who had accumulated

about fifty trophies in five years, I needed a *backup plan*. It

always sounded very cliché' when older people used the term,

but after researching the statistics, I accepted the fact that my

odds were extremely low despite my basketball talent. There

was a daily battle with myself as to whether or not I was

prematurely giving up, and I often wondered would my parents

be disappointed if I were never able to buy them a mansion

because I gave up on my hoop dreams. On the other hand, I

would think of all the guys I knew who were well into their late

twenties and thirties who were still *hoop dreaming* with no

backup plan. I decided I could live with the price of not making it

to the NBA, but I could not live with the price of not being able to

free myself from the Trap.

The candle was now lit within me. I researched careers

that paid $80,000-$ 100,000 per year. The salary was an

important factor, but the ability to move out of the Trap

relatively quickly was paramount. I researched becoming a

doctor, although I knew a C+ average in high school minimized

that possibility. The total amount of years required to become a

physician canceled out that profession since finances would

require me to remain in the Trap for another seven years. I was

uncertain I could remain alive and sane for another 7 years in the

Trap. Besides, how would I have possibly been able to focus on a

high enough level when dealing with all the negative factors of

living in the Trap? Perhaps if my parents were wealthy, I might

have indeed been able to have the initials MD behind my last name. All the information I gathered made me determined to figure out the most lucrative profession with the shortest duration I would study and soon realized many professions required only one or two years of post-high school education. This math meant with a little hard work, I could be making $80.000-$100,000 a year by the time I was twenty-one, and I could escape the Trap by twenty-five!

> Since the rent in was pretty low in the housing projects, I knew if I could stay focused and maximize my resources, I would be able to save a ton of money to finance my escape from the Trap a lot sooner.

I was extremely fortunate not to have a criminal record by twenty years old, as many of my peers did. My path seemed much clearer, and it was time to escape the Trap. Due to the number of funeral homes located in my neighborhood and research on salaries, I settled on studying to become a mortician. The program was two years long, and the earning potential was high. Some of my friends were serving two to five-year prison sentences, so I figured if they could handle two to five years in prison; I surely could handle two additional years of school. I went to a mortuary school in Atlanta for two years but decided the unpredictable schedule required to be a mortician was not a good fit for my personality. I resisted with all the energy I had but unfortunately was forced to return to Harlem and reassess my life. I was extremely disappointed and began to wonder if I would become part of the percentage that never escapes. I made a contract with myself to have a viable means of income by twenty-five years old. This promise bought me enough time to finally see the black cloud cease from hovering over me and the sun to begin shining on my life. After taking a one-year break from school, I decided to study radiology. I completed the two-year program, and at twenty-four years old was making $80,000 a year. At times I was amazed at the fact I was so young and making that much money from going to school for two years. I would pick up extra shifts to be paid overtime on a regular basis. This allowed me to expedite my escape. I would often go to the bank to deposit my paycheck, and there was an attractive bank teller who for about eighteen months, I never had the opportunity to *land on*.

I would always attempt to make eye contact with her while waiting in line with no success. One Friday afternoon, the opportunity finally presented itself for her to assist me with my transaction. Although she purposely never once noticed me in the past, as she entered my information into the computer my account balance appeared, her eyes grew wider, and she immediately asked me "what are you doing tonight?" Making $80,000 per year for two consecutive years and saving most of it provided for her astonished reaction. I figured I stood out because there probably were not too many young African American men with large savings at this bank. This moment provided validation for all the hard work and patience; I exhibited up until this point in my life.

I curved her advance because she was obviously more interested in my account balance than my morals or personality.

I figured there would be many more attractive women to choose from in the future who did not have knowledge of my account balance and my assumption was correct.

This was also a further vindication of my decision to make selling drugs my absolute last resort rather than the first. I knew, barring some asinine decision on my part, I had now practically escaped the Trap forever.

This ideology created a glaring contrast between many of my peers and me. A good portion of my friends began to sell drugs early in life, partly because of greed but mostly due to hopelessness. If you tell a teenager he has a high probability of making $50,000 a year legally by the age of twenty-five if he chooses not to sell drugs, he probably will listen. However, in the Trap we all simply strived just to make it to twenty-five, so seeing the next year or day was the priority. We were young, and many of us decided –just as I did with my lawsuit scheme- that illegal activity was the first approach we would consider as a means of escaping or at a minimum making life in the Trap more bearable.

A good portion of us were blessed with God-given talents we never had the chance to take advantage of. We were not only talented at sports or entertainment. Many of us could have been psychologists, screenwriters, or owned successful businesses. Due to the environment, we resided in, it was necessary to be aware of individuals' body language and overall characteristics. We became incredibly good at knowing when someone wasn't feeling too great about life or concealing a bald-faced lie, strictly from observing facial expressions and posture. In the Trap, the term *"keep it real,"* was used so often because it is difficult to conceal emotions. You were obligated to keep it real a majority of the time.

Some of the other guys were the most comedic characters you could ever find. We would have snapping sessions where we would make jokes about everything from each other's mothers to how financially broke an individual was. In my opinion, the writers from *Seinfeld* or *Saturday Night Live* had nothing on these guys. I remember one summer when a guy's dog ran into traffic and was killed. He and his dog had been inseparable, and everyone realized how much grief he had to be enduring. We were standing on our usual corner as the news spread through the neighborhood and at the exact moment all of us were expressing sympathy for his loss- with impeccable timing one of the funniest guys in the neighborhood couldn't help but say" oh well, all dogs go to heaven." Everyone wholeheartedly attempted to resist bursting out in laughter, but in the end, the joke was just so well timed the outburst of laughter was uncontrollable. This individual was also able to receive the jokes just as well as he dished them out. He was very dark skinned and always wore the latest designer clothes. During one of our snapping sessions, his cousin reminded him that he was nothing more than a "fancy cab driver." Many of the cab drivers in NYC are from sub-Saharan Africa. Therefore, they have very dark complexions. These two jokes which I still remember twenty years later are prime examples of the talent we could tap into if we rejected the lies society has conditioned us to accept about our destinies. He did not need to attend a prestigious performing arts school; the environment naturally created this humor-but also prevented it from flourishing.

Most of us were also somewhat financially savvy. Due to our limited resources, we would muster a day's worth of food on about six or seven dollars. Our favorite meal was the three dollar turkey and cheese sandwich on a roll with a bag of chips and a fifty-cent soda. Our sandwiches were so filling because we made sure the guy made the sandwiches the same way every time and sliced the turkey pieces as thick as we wanted. The fifty-cent soda was rumored to cause sterility in males, so we named it a "nut buster." This rumor was never verified as fact, but even as it floated throughout the neighborhood, we never ceased drinking it since the price and taste were so good. We also would often share our food. If you were the first to come on the block with a cheeseburger from the local chicken spot, it was almost always guaranteed someone would say "let me get a piece of that." Before you knew it, half of your sandwich was gone before you ever had a chance to take a bite. I quickly realized I would be better off eating my food and drink in the chicken spot or the park behind my building before returning to the block. You were often even asked to share some of your "nut buster"-so not only did you have to worry about not being able to reproduce, but you also were forced to swap spit. In retrospect, I wonder how any of us ever enjoyed our food in peace. This nuance was really irritating but became less prevalent as we grew older.

While we never bought into the myth about the fifty-cent soda making us unable to reproduce, many of us, including myself, bought into the myth which leads you to admire the most negative characteristics of the Trap. When I was in junior high school, I can remember having arguments with kids from other housing projects about whose neighborhood was worse. We would refer to statistics like murders and robberies to validate our admiration. I can remember having an argument with my friend, who lived in the Abraham Lincoln Projects located on the east side of Harlem. We went back and forth for about an hour, and the conversation went like this "You are crazy man, my projects has way more killers than yours, we got shit in the staircase and everything, the elevators stay pissy, and we had like five shootouts this summer, your projects ain't have shit, y' all only have nice old ladies over there, y' all ain't as real as us."

I had grown so conditioned to love the very things that made my projects a difficult place to live that I must have had possibly ten to twenty of these debates with various friends throughout my early teenage years. This conditioning was partly due to the more dangerous your neighborhood was the more respect you received from your peers.

There was an incident that exemplified this phenomenon while visiting some girls in the St. Nicholas projects on a cold winter night when the guys from their projects were contemplating robbing us. It was unbeknownst to us until one of the girls volunteered this information. As soon as we entered the projects people were looking out the windows seemingly waiting to see what was going to happen. As the guys approached us, one of them asked, "Where y' all from?"

A few of us replied, "Drew Hamilton."

The only other word the guy said was, "okay."
After this, everyone dispersed, and it was clear that where we were from caused them to reconsider their scheme since they respected the high probability, there would be retaliation for any attempt to harm us.

The geographic layout of the projects on the west side of Harlem also played a factor on this night. Once you passed 125th Street and 8th Avenue traveling uptown there is the St. Nicholas

Projects, Drew Hamilton Projects, and the Polo Grounds Towers where the famed Rucker Basketball tournament is held every summer. These housing projects are each separated by about ten New York City blocks. Unless you took a detour, to get to the Rucker Tournament, you had to walk past the block we hung out on. In instances like these, it did pay to be from a known neighborhood; however, I wish the gangster factor was less relevant so we could improve the standard of living in our community. I would much rather live in a peaceful, clean neighborhood than have to promote the negativity of my neighborhood for protection.

The negative factors of crime, garbage, drug addicts, urine-filled elevators, and human feces in the staircases were constants in all of the housing projects I had ever visited. One afternoon, my sister and I were having a debate as to whether these negative factors actually existed in every housing project. My sister, who worked for social services, informed me she had an eye opening experience of visiting two separate housing projects in Brooklyn that did not have the negative factors common to most other housing projects. As she shared her detailed description, it was as if she was speaking of an undiscovered planet. She continued on with details of how the staircases were well lit, the front door locks and intercom weren't broken, and there weren't any urine filled elevators. I resisted the information she was providing and continued to insist she must have been confused. These must have been co-ops or some other housing which she mistakenly thought were New York City Housing Authority complexes. As the debate continued, she solidified her argument by stating the names of the developments along with photo evidence of the distinct blue and orange signs which were located at the entrance of all New York City Housing projects at the time. The two housing projects were called Williams *Plaza* and *Independence Towers*. These two housing projects consisted of an eighty percent Hasidic Jewish population. I immediately had a sense of curiosity as to why I'd never heard of nice housing projects where mostly African Americans resided.

I instantly began comparing different characteristics of the two vastly different neighborhoods. As I made my comparisons, I quickly gravitated toward the financial differences which I falsely assumed existed. I thought, of course, that in the Hasidic Jewish housing project, residents must be far more financially stable than African Americans residing in public housing. I presented my emotional, hasty reply to my sister, and she again disproved my theory by confirming that many of the Hasidic residents were on some form of public assistance. Once I accepted the statistics, she presented me, feelings of enlightenment and disappointment began to come over me. I was excited to learn of a public housing Heaven and simultaneously disappointed as to why most of us African Americans and Latinos were trapped in a public housing hell.

In my projects, living on the second floor meant we couldn't open our windows in the summertime even though there was no central air due to the fear of giant rats entering our apartment from the windowsill. The garbage was often not collected for days, and the lids on the trash cans were left open for rats to feast. I remember going to the management office to complain and was told I should close the lid on the trash cans if I did not want the rat problem to get worse. These are further examples of the hell we so gracefully resided in. I was familiar with a quote which states, "cleanliness is next to godliness."

Were the Hasidic Jews godlier therefore valued their neighborhood more?

Since there were churches on almost every few blocks in Harlem, I rationalized the answer was indeed no. I am fairly certain the moment the first sign of their neighborhood deteriorating appeared, the Hasidic Jewish residents would have confronted these problems immediately. For some reason, we allowed them to fester to a point in which this became our accepted standard of living.

My search for answers regarding such a disparity once again led me down the path of the four-hundred-year history of slavery and segregation suffered by African Americans in the

United States. In my research, I quickly linked the sub-human conditions of slave quarters, segregated accommodations, and segregated neighborhoods to the dilapidated conditions of many African American neighborhoods. Perhaps we had subconsciously grown to love living in the struggle. Having a normal standard of living was maybe foreign to our collective minds, and over time, we grew more comfortable in uncomfortable situations.

This analysis helped me understand why we so irrationally loved to boast about the negative aspects of our neighborhoods so much more than the positives. Rejecting this myth, which has conditioned us to accept the blight of our communities allowed my mind to be set free. The truth is— there is absolutely nothing wrong with expecting to live in a safe, peaceful community; the lie is wanting to do so somehow makes you a weak person who is selling out to the so called "man".

Many of us buy into this myth for years until we have kids of our own. I have seen children change the perspective of some of the toughest, ignorant individuals. The problem is, by the time they actually realized they have been tricked into failure, their lives have usually been irreversibly minimized to the point they will never reach a fraction of their God-given potential. Instead of giving the next generation a head start, this mentality leaves them to start life at the same point or even further behind than the previous. It's sort of like buying into a Ponzi scheme in which you believe you are making a fantastic investment, receiving great returns only to find out the joke was on you the entire time and you have been irretrievably damaged.

The anger those of us tricked into loving the Trap should be far greater than those who have fallen victim to Ponzi schemes. I certainly suffered feelings of anger from being bamboozled for a period, but also took solace in the fact that I was able to gain an understanding of the truth which would eventually set my mind and my life free.

As I watched television and continued to analyze the disparities in the living conditions of those in the ghetto compared to those in middle-class America, I began to notice an eerily similar pattern. The pattern was that many of the dilapidated African American neighborhoods across the country were very aesthetically similar to other comparable neighborhoods. After my eye-opening conversation with my sister, I now analyzed for disparities in neighborhoods with similar aesthetics even closer. I soon noticed a far greater disparity of two neighborhoods, which I was told were owned by the same company. The construction and design of the two communities make it easy to realize they are indeed sister properties. These two neighborhoods are called *Waterside Plaza* and *River Park Towers*. Waterside Plaza is a luxury high-rise community consisting of four buildings located off the East River on 25th street in Lower Manhattan. This community has underground parking, a playground, an Olympic size swimming pool, spa, gorgeous views of the East River, and is located directly across the street from several hospitals as well. The rents for these apartments ranged between $2000 per month for a studio apartment to $10000 per month for a townhouse style unit.

If Waterside Plaza and River Park Towers are twin properties, River Park Towers could be considered the evil twin. Located in the Morris Heights section of the South Bronx, River Park Towers is also a four-building apartment development with underground parking, a playground, access to Olympic size swimming pool, gorgeous views of the Harlem River and the George Washington Bridge. However, a visit to these two communities will allow your mind's eye to register the glaring disparity instantly. Entering River Park Towers on even the sunniest days, you immediately notice the sun does not shine quite as bright as it does in Waterside Plaza for some odd reason. The feeling of entering a danger zone sets upon you well before you arrive at the security gate at the entrance of the development. There are seventeen hundred apartments and six thousand documented residents, but the six thousand number is definitely low. Out of the six

thousand residents, I would estimate about one hundred to two

hundred dudes were hanging out in front of the four buildings on

any given night. I once dated a female whose sister lived in River

Park Towers, and every time I visited, it would feel as though I

was playing Russian roulette with my safety.

When driving, I would simply wait for my girlfriend to

come downstairs since I could not risk leaving my car idle for

even a mere ten minutes. I had heard stories of eggs, batteries,

and countless other things including refrigerators being thrown

from the windows damaging vehicles left unattended. During the

times I visited by taking the train or a taxicab, the feelings of

uneasiness were still present but were definitely diminished due

to being able to blend in more easily. Essentially driving in

immediately painted you as an outsider while walking allowed

you to appear a commoner to the neighborhood. There was still

a risk involved because if any confrontation occurred while you

were on foot, you probably would not make it out of the

complex. Since even law-abiding citizens are not allowed to carry firearms in New York City, I chose to drive every time after my first visit there. I would try to avoid going there, but since my girlfriend loved to visit her sister, I was obligated by default if I wanted to hang out with her.

The striking contrast between the two neighborhoods would frustrate me as to why River Park Towers could not be as inviting as Waterside Plaza. Whenever I would visit River Park Towers, I could not help but think about how different I would feel if I were picking her up from Waterside Plaza instead. This experience also again caused me to question why life was so difficult for those of us who resided in the Trap.

As a teenager, I remember watching movies like

Boyz N Da Hood, *Colors*, and *Menace to Society*, which are urban classics. I have personally seen each at least ten times. These movies documented the lives of African Americans in beautiful Los Angeles, California. My mind was captivated by the

sunshine, palm trees, and the portrayal of African Americans

living in houses. For me, this was a huge step up from growing up

in the projects of New York City. I would have been willing to

trade many things to grow up in a house as a teen. As I learned

more about the many trials and tribulations of those living in the

areas portrayed in these movies, I realized I wouldn't want to

make the trade of living in my projects. The grass literally seemed

greener but clearly wasn't as you took a closer look. If there

could not be peace and harmony in tree-lined, sun-filled, owner-

occupied neighborhoods where could it possibly exist for African

Americans?

I struggled to find a single thriving neighborhood

throughout the entire world which was predominantly

populated by people of the darker hue. Watching the

classic films about African American life in Los Angeles

changed my perception that the Trap was only an

American living condition, I was now convinced escaping

the Trap was a worldwide struggle and should be the number one priority for all of those born with a darker hue. From the hundreds of housing projects in New York City to the gang infested neighborhoods of Los Angeles to the shanty towns of South Africa, you will find a common theme of darker skinned people born into an environment that required them to spend a good portion of their lives trying to escape from it. Rather than being able to live comfortably within our neighborhoods, we were forced to cope with living uncomfortably while most of those with lighter skin were afforded the luxury of living life in an oasis rather than a desert.

While living in the Trap was uncomfortable, I came to understand it certainly didn't nearly compare to the shanty towns in South Africa or the slums in Mumbai, India. All of us had shoes to put on our feet and clothing for our backs. Not only did we have the essentials, but most of us also had excess. We had numerous pairs of Air Jordans, Timberland boots, and $400

North Face jackets which kept us warm in the winter when we

hung out on the corners. In fact, all of our clothing was name

brand and often designer. There were these $250 Gore-Tex snow

boots called A-SOLOS which were popular during my era and at

least ten of us in a five-block radius owned a pair, including me.

These examples prove most of us were not in fact

financially poor but mostly mentally poor. The luxuries of

having designer clothes and $250 boots made me feel

good to be in the upper echelon of my community, but

whenever I traveled below 96th Street, those feelings

quickly transformed into feelings of inadequacy and

inequity. The inequities caused me to appreciate that we

weren't truly poor but poor in relation to others. When I

fully absorbed this rationale, it aided me in realizing my

neighborhood was actually fertile ground for me to

obtain financial stability. Low-cost housing, combined

with an above average salary at a young age, should

surely wipe away the inequity in five years or less. Society and the news media instilled in us that we were poor and underprivileged; however, I now understood I was, in fact, privileged to live in an environment which essentially allowed me to start my adult financial life with a head start and erase the inequities I was born into. They say turning a negative to a positive makes for a better picture. This was certainly true in my case.

I learned in school how all races suffering injustices received some form of reparations from their oppressors except for black people. Therefore, I was now determined to use my neighborhoods' low cost of living to grant myself reparations, putting me on equal footing with someone who inherited generational wealth.

I imagined what if one hundred guys in my immediate neighborhood followed the same road map how drastically my neighborhood would be forever transformed for the better. I asked myself, which is better, a neighborhood where one person becomes a

millionaire every few years or one which one hundred

people make $50,000-$100,000 every year?

It was a rhetorical question since many *individuals*

have achieved a level of success that allowed them to

escape the Trap. However, the neighborhoods have yet

to improve despite individual successes.

The prospect of one hundred of my peers earning

yearly salaries of $50,000-$100,000 a year was a great

thing to envision; however, it was a long shot. The odds

were long due to another myth that many of us as a

community embraced during the 1980s and 1990s. So

many of us believed going to prison was a greater badge

of honor than going to school. If you served more than

five years in prison, you were viewed with an almost folk

hero type of mystique. This mindset continues to keep

young urban youth in mental slavery, which eventually

materializes into real life slavery. I use the term slavery

because after I learned about the shackles placed on slaves as a child, I vowed I would do everything in my power to never be placed in any kind of chains mental or physical. This perspective also allowed my mind to be set free from the Trap. I was and forever will be allergic to handcuffs. Once I learned the history of my ancestors, I grew certain they couldn't have possibly expended so much energy breaking free from the shackles of slavery to have later generations turn around and accept that being held captive in any capacity was appealing. Unfortunately, many of us did find being incarcerated appealing and something to aspire to. As twisted as it may sound, it was one hundred percent absolutely true. The badge of honor of being incarcerated would cause many of us to brag about our cousin, brother, or uncle who was currently or previously incarcerated.

We would mention it to others with a grin full of pride. It was as if the incarcerated individual was an astronaut who went on a space mission. Although we recognized he would be in *outer space* for the near future, a part of us was still prideful that he could withstand such a mission.

I remember a time where I had an argument with a guy from my projects in which he challenged my character because I hadn't done any jail time. He stated, "you ain't a real nigga; you ain't never worn no state greens or seen the inside of no jail."

As my temperature began to rise and my blood began boiling, I took in a deep breath and rationalized that I was arguing with someone who was questioning my integrity because I HAD YET TO KNOW THE FEELING OF BEING CAGED AND SHACKLED. In essence, he wanted me to know what it feels like to be a slave and resented me for choosing to bypass that experience.

His mind, body, and soul clearly had grown to love the Trap and desperately needed to escape.

I took in a deep breath and replied, "So I'm not real cause

I NEVER WANT TO LIVE LIKE A SLAVE? THE ANCESTORS ALREADY

LIVED THAT SO I DON'T HAVE TO HOMIE."

He remained quiet momentarily, clearly lacking a valid

response. Then he said, "Why you always trying to school

somebody on some shit? Nobody wanna hear that."

This statement crystallizes the ideology even I

admittedly adopted for a period of my life. Previously, I

simply wouldn't allow my mind to be set free just as he

refused to. Prior to being enlightened, I had more

respect for the hustler than the working man, the guy

who did ten years in jail than the kid who returned to the

neighborhood from college, the stick up kid than the nine

to five worker, and the girl who did check scams to earn

money than the mom who remained legit raising two kids

alone while taking night time college classes.

We revered the thief more than the earner.

As my mind expanded with maturity, I began to realize being a thief all your life didn't mean you were crafty or outwitted the system as many of us thought, it simply meant you were a loser who hadn't obtained the success in your life which would allow you to buy the things you wanted.

One of the saddest things to see is a thirty-five-year-old career criminal who has to plot and scheme every day of his life to survive. He wakes up looking for the next score and even if you're close friends with him, you can't trust him for even one minute. This type of individual will hang on to anyone in the neighborhood who appears to be on the verge of success as a means of escaping his pathetic life. He constantly tells stories about all the people he robbed as if these capers really improved his life. I used to listen to these stories as I stood on my block and would quietly think to myself, "this dude is gonna either be out here telling these stories for the next twenty years, or he's gonna get killed."

My logic was always this—after years of risking his life committing crimes, there should have been some progression of his standard of living. I equated his situation to running on a hamster wheel. In the grand reality of things, his actions weren't advancing his life, and he would eventually run out of breath and fall right off his hamster wheel. There were countless individuals similar to him who by the time they'd reached forty years old were filled with war stories and regrets.

Once I became aware of the playbook of myths that infiltrated black communities and caused so much grief for so many African Americans, I realized our suffering has continued for so many years due to repeatedly believing these proven to fail myths would eventually lead us to success.

In the National Football League, Tom Brady would never continue to call a play that never succeeded. His profound success as a quarterback is due to having the ability to analyze the opponents' schemes to disrupt his plans and consequently call a play that disrupts their plans. In my community, we continued to embrace the plays which we've already witnessed fail generation after generation.

Armed with the strong suspicion our inability to improve these conditions was mostly a mental issue rather than a physical ailment, I pondered almost daily why I was born into such as rough substandard environment which was unable to change. Due to frustration, I became determined to undertake a self-study program as to what were the dominant ideologies which had been so successful in stifling improvement of African American neighborhoods throughout America for multiple generations and vowed to eventually rid my thought process of all of them.

I vowed to reject the notion we were poor; in my eyes, this is the first step in demoralizing a person and making them feel inferior. We were less privileged in relation to other races in

America, but we were far better off than those kids born into the villages of Africa or slums in India. I can't think of a single day throughout my life when I couldn't find even a slice of bread to eat. Also, our neighborhood was rich with spontaneous fun and laughter during periods when violence wasn't prevalent.

Our neighborhoods were more fun and fuller of life due to everyone being outside and interacting all the time.

Rejecting the notion, we were poor allowed me to reject the mentality that I needed to sell drugs as a means to accumulate wealth. I think many African Americans born into the Trap have a perception that all Caucasian people are financially well off and many Caucasians born into privilege perceive most African Americans as being poor. I had come to learn neither of these was true. There were many Caucasians who were only able to live in affluent areas of New York City by sharing two-bedroom apartments with five people, and there were individuals in my projects who had a two-bedroom apartment and worked for the New York City Transit Authority earning over $70,000 a year.

I also looked at the less privileged Chinese immigrants residing in China Town. I was certain many of them were less fortunate than us, and if they weren't desperate enough to sell drugs to their own people, then I definitely shouldn't be either. Their underprivileged condition also didn't cause them to shoot and kill each other on a regular basis, so therefore our underprivileged conditions shouldn't be an excuse for us to do it. This, in turn, allowed me to realize robbing and stealing from my own community also weren't necessary evils. This thread of epiphanies aided me in removing the drug dealer; stick up kid, and murderer from my mental pedestal. I gradually grew to admire the one percent of those who were able to avoid all the pitfalls of the Trap and escape virtually unscathed.

I began to admire stories of individuals who were able to escape without sports, entertainment, and crime whereas in the past, I was more intrigued by these triumphs. My mentality underwent a complete metamorphosis towards the truth, and in the end, it

would be these truths which aided in setting me free from the

Trap once and for all.

Rebirth

Soon after my mind was emancipated, my physical surroundings followed suit.

The places I found myself frequenting were far different than those during my earlier years. The atmospheres were more relaxed, and people weren't on edge. It was obvious I entered a new dimension of life in which I was now free from both real and imaginary restrictions. The world was now mine to explore as I saw fit.

The process of physically freeing myself accelerated one snowy morning after returning from a long overnight shift at a hospital in Brooklyn. The previous night when I left for work, I saw one of the guys from my neighborhood sitting on a milk crate on the corner of my project building. A snowstorm passed through the tri-state area, which ended early the next morning. As I was crossing the street toward my building, to my surprise and disappointment, he was still sitting on the same crate in the same spot as the night before. Although I was exhausted from work and the one-hour train ride home, I was nearly compelled to educate him due to the blend of emotions I was feeling at that moment.

I immediately viewed my witnessing him still sitting on the milk crate as a sign it was now the time to free myself and my family from the Trap. Feelings of empathy and sadness for him also came to me as well due to the fact we grew up together, yet the direction our lives appeared to be headed couldn't have been any more polar opposite.

This encounter triggered feelings of survivor's guilt as I asked myself, "How did I do it?

Why was he satisfied sitting on a milk crate all day? What was the difference?"

Just a few years prior, I too sat on milk crates all night to the next morning on the corners of Harlem nearly every day just like him. Therefore, I wasn't casting judgment on him. I was merely thinking to myself, "if he only knew how successful I'm on the verge of becoming and the fact I'm no longer sitting on the corner all night aided in my newfound success, he probably would give up sitting on the corner all day and night as well."

As I got closer to him, he noticed I was wearing green hospital scrubs, and he asked me,

"Yo my brother, you work in a hospital kid?"

I replied, "yeah, man, it's a beautiful thing."

I thought for a moment to pull him to the side and breakdown how much money I was making from completing a two-year program. I resisted the urge, however. My street smarts told me not to divulge such sensitive financial information. Plus, I was certain he would think that my path wasn't necessarily for him.

Before this moment, even though I had saved up more than enough money to ensure my family would never have to return to the Trap, I had grown complacent due to living there

for so long. I figured since I've survived the Trap for twenty years,

one or two more years couldn't hurt. However, in the Trap, one

more day, month, or year could mean life or death.

This chance encounter woke me up in a sense. It was now time

to move below 96th Street, a nice section of Queens, a suburb in

New Jersey, or anywhere outside of the Trap for that matter.

I sat in the house all day and reflected on all the sacrifices

made by my parents and me to have this opportunity to be a

part of the New York City everyone sees on TV , rather than

being forever trapped in an environment many people choose to

place in the most posterior portion of their minds. I was now on

the verge of being in the middle of the bright lights of the big

city.

After recovering from my overnight shift through some

great sleep, that same afternoon, I immediately proceeded to

search for a new place for me and my mom. My concern was less

about me and more about her since my ultimate plan to escape from the Trap was to move to Atlanta in a few years. I had navigated the Trap well for more than twenty years; therefore, I was pretty seasoned. I simply couldn't fathom leaving my mom behind while I was living a great life in Atlanta. At the very least, I knew I owed her an improved standard of living for all the correct decisions she made in her life prior to and after she birthed me.

This was the primary fuel that gave me the newfound urgency to relocate her. After researching a few co-ops and condos in the Murray Hill section of Manhattan, I took in a deep breath, closed my eyes, and asked God to release us from the Trap.

My dad always told me God will help you as long as you help yourself.

Living in Murray Hill would have required I spend at least $2,500 per month on a studio apartment or obtain a $500,000 mortgage which my mom wouldn't be able to afford in the event something bad happened to me. I was confident God would answer my prayers since I was certain I had made all of the right decisions deserving of a better life, such as avoiding confrontations when possible, resisting temptations of fast money, no longer wasting time on the corners, learning a craft, working many hours per week, and sometimes traveling in snowstorms to work at far away hospitals.

I debated whether I should abandon my dreams of moving to Atlanta and just stay with my mom in New York City for as long as necessary. Amazingly, before I could become obligated to a large mortgage for thirty years and within two weeks of my encounter with my friend and my prayer- we received a letter from one of the apartments I applied to. This apartment was located on 56th Street and 10th Avenue.

The day I checked the mail, saw the letter, and opened it; I couldn't believe my eyes. It happened so quickly I initially thought it was a prank or solicitation, but realized it was authentic when I referenced back to my prayer request. I could feel a rebirth was soon to occur.

My future seemed as bright as the sun. In essence, my real life was about to begin, whereas my old life wasn't quite a nightmare but definitely a bad dream.

For my mom, however, this news was a fantasy come true. She had grown tired of the human feces in the staircases, and tired of working hard yet not being able to live in a suitable area. Despite being exhausted by project living, she was even more skeptical about the good news than I was. I remember her saying, "they are just trying to trick me into giving up my three-bedroom apartment and then they are going to give me an apartment I can't afford on my own, then I'm going to have nowhere to live."

She doubled down and decided she wasn't going to move anywhere.

We battled over this for three weeks, and we were only

given thirty days to decide if we were going to accept the

apartment. As my mom continued to resist the possibility that

moving out of the projects was now indeed a reality, I'd come to

grasp an opportunity of this magnitude to live a few blocks away

from the Time Warner building probably wouldn't come around

ever again. The Time Warner building is located on Columbus

Circle, one of the best addresses known to Manhattan. The time

for endless debate and fear had come to an end; it was now time

to devise a scheme to get my mom to leave our apartment for

just a few days. This was all the time I needed to hire movers and

get all our stuff out of our soon to be former living quarters.

I proceeded to conjure up a plan with my sister, who

bought a house on the border of Long Island a few years earlier

after returning from the Army. We decided to lure my mom over

to her house for a weekend staycation. Naturally, my mom being

the feisty woman she was, initially resisted the offer with every

fiber in her body until we shamed her under the guise of not spending enough quality time with the family. After numerous attempts during that week, my mom finally agreed to spend a few days with my sister.

My mom unknowingly signed the acceptance letter and I swiftly mailed it to the apartment management office.

Escaping the Trap was closer than ever to becoming a reality.

This taste of freedom I imagined was similar to how the slaves felt when they made it into free territory but to a lesser degree since we weren't being physically held captive. Despite not being held captive physically, those residing in the Trap were captives of a system that allows lower level standards of living and the bittersweet taste cannot be understated.

Nonetheless, I was far more focused on maximizing my new existence than reminiscing on the constraints of my past life.

Once my sister whisked my mom away from home, I wasted no time in beginning to pack up dishes, silverware, pictures, and all the hundreds of keepsakes my mom

accumulated over the years in our cluttered apartment. By the

third day of staying at my sister's house, my mom started fussing

and insisted she be brought back home immediately. The movers

weren't scheduled to begin until the fifth day, but I was able to

get the date moved up by promising generous tips. The clock was

ticking, my mom returning home was simply not an option as she

would almost certainly sabotage the entire opportunity by

refusing to move out. I knew my sister could only hold her for so

long. If mom continued to make a fuss, my sister would give in

and bring her home.

The night before the movers were scheduled to come, I

single handedly attempted to throw out all non-important items

to guarantee my mom would receive her security deposit back

from the New York City Housing Authority. However, as the night

went on and the task became increasingly daunting, I gave up

and decided since I had a nice nest egg saved, a few hundred

dollars was no longer worth the effort I was putting in to leave the apartment in move in condition in order to receive the two hundred fifty dollar security deposit.

I made at least fifty trips up and down the stairs; luckily, we only lived on the second floor. As I made my numerous trips to the garbage dump, it became obvious to the whole neighborhood we were moving out soon. There were a mix of reactions. Crack heads were literally waiting by the garbage dump for me to bring more stuff down. Associates of mine passing by questioned, "You moving my nigga? You one lucky nigga!"

I didn't want them in my business, so I simply replied, "Nah, just throwing some stuff out."

To friends whom I trusted a bit more, I replied, "Yeah, I'm moving and never coming back."

For the others who chose not to acknowledge what they were seeing, we had no interaction.

Seeing the crack heads waiting by the dumpster for the items I was throwing away was quite a sight. One of them asked me about one particular item, "You really just gonna throw that away?" It was as if he were certain he could auction it off one day and end up on Antiques Roadshow.

His question caused me to hesitate and consider taking this particular item out of the trash since it might be valuable, but again I was simply ready to leave all things from my restricted life in the past. I let him keep it.

I didn't finish removing all the items from the apartment until nine o'clock that night.

I was exhausted and decided to get a good night's rest because I knew the next day was going to be a day like I had never experienced before. I wanted all my senses heightened so that I could fully absorb this life-changing transition.

The next day was bright and sunny. It was a weekday in the middle of spring, and the neighborhood was active with people going about their normal business. I woke up and went downstairs to get one last taste of the neighborhood before the movers arrived. This was the neighborhood I'd grown accustomed to and loved so much yet knew I had to leave in order to have a better life. It was a conscious decision to get up early because I understood I wouldn't have the relative peace and quiet to fully absorb the moment later in the day once everyone began hanging out on the corner and the movers had arrived.

When I made it downstairs, I looked up the block towards 7th Avenue and down the block towards 8th Avenue. I looked up at the sky then towards the basketball courts where so many of my neighborhood memories reside, took in a big deep breath, let out a sigh of relief, and walked to the corner store to buy the homemade chocolate chip cookies I loved so much, probably for the last time.

These cookies were a neighborhood staple; you could smell them baking as you walked by the store, and if you waited more than a half hour to buy some, they were usually gone. I savored them more than ever because often the hood is where you find some of the best hidden gems and my new neighborhood would probably only carry some high-end brand which didn't taste nearly as good.

I thought to myself, "Oh well, in life you usually have to give up something to get something."

While these cookies were delicious, it wasn't only the memories of the taste I was seeking to hold onto. It was the memories of my mom coming home at midnight from a hard day cleaning hotel rooms but still stopping at the corner store to buy some and us eating them together before I went to sleep. It was also the memories of standing on the corners for hours during the cold winters and how eating these cookies momentarily allowed you to forget how cold it really was. It was also the countless walks me and my friends took in order buy these cookies. They were more than just cookies. For me, they were a symbol of good in an often bad place. That's why I treasured them so much.

We are often led to believe good things don't exist in urban neighborhoods, yet I knew with fair certainty this was one thing that we were privileged to have that the kids in more affluent neighborhoods weren't.

After spending about fifteen minutes in front of my building reminiscing about the days of old, it was now time to head back upstairs and prepare for the moment the movers arrived. I paced around the apartment and must have looked out the window at least twenty times.

Our windows looked out onto the park behind the building, which we ingeniously called the *Back* Park. This view also faced toward 142nd and 8th Avenue—the block I hung out on almost every day for about ten years. Again, as I drifted into a daze, more questions arose. I contemplated the effects of leaving old memories and friendships behind. Was I somehow abandoning those who taught me how to swim and ride a bike? Would there forever be a hole in my heart created by essentially amputating myself from my old life? Should I go to the block to tell all those who I had admiration for and who held admiration for me, I was leaving never to return? Could I have done more by guiding close friends down the same path I traveled by keeping them close to me, so this moment could have consisted of more than just me escaping the Trap?

I was rapidly spiraling into more and more questions. My emotions were beginning to overtake me. So, rather than waste another forty-five minutes in a daze, I decided to block out all emotions until everything was moved out of the apartment. I spent the next hour or so doing the final preparations and then the phone rang. It was the movers notifying me they were in route and would be at my building in fifteen minutes. I began to have feelings of peace and triumph come over me, and for that moment, all the things I pondered over just a few minutes prior became insignificant.

I realized that I truly had beaten the odds and avoided becoming a statistic despite being immersed in and embracing the trap.

There was a knock on the door exactly fifteen minutes later as the movers promised. I gathered my composure before opening the door and introduced myself. The lead mover quickly observed how everything was strategically organized and said, "Man, you made our job really easy. I can tell by the grin on your face and how well you've organized everything, you must really want to get out of here."

I replied, "Yeah, it's been a long time coming. I've waited for this day for twenty years, and it's almost as if I'm dreaming. When my family moved in here, it was a dark night, and now, we are moving out on a perfect sunny day."

By this time, a few of the usual neighborhood guys were hanging on the corner of my building. As the movers began making their trips up and down the stairs, I accompanied them on several trips to supervise what they were doing. I was hesitant at first since I expected many questions would be coming my way from the neighborhood guys. The last thing I wanted was for someone to ask if I hit the lottery or won a lawsuit, but it was understandable since the move appeared so sudden and there aren't too many people who make it out by other means. To my surprise, even with all the boxes, furniture, and moving trucks, very few people chose to acknowledge what was occurring, willfully or not.

In my twenty years of living in the projects, it was rare to see a moving truck, and if you did it was usually a family moving in. I expected to run into a hater or two, but the move was completed uneventfully. It was as if the universe was allowing me to have total peace in this moment which I'd worked so hard for over the past twenty years by always seeking to evade the pitfalls of the Trap.

The move out was complete, and now I was required to meet the movers at our new midtown Manhattan apartment.

When I reiterated the location, we were moving to I could see the lead mover had acquired a high level of respect for me from the look in his eyes and the firmness of his handshake. He seemed aware that what he was witnessing doesn't happen every day or even every year.

I went back upstairs one final time, closed my eyes, took in the biggest breath I could, and thanked God for granting me this moment.

It wasn't lost on me that there are people who would literally kill for the opportunity to live in the heart of Manhattan.

An hour later, I arrived at the new building a few minutes ahead of the moving crew, granting me a small opportunity to absorb my new lifestyle. While I was aware of all that living in a nice neighborhood had to offer, to actually be there absorbing the atmosphere was far different than fantasizing about the experience.

Yellow taxi cabs were all over. Young ladies were walking their poodles and Maltese's. The air was much fresher; the breeze from the Hudson River was constant. Flowers were planted along the street, and the tree branches swayed in the wind similar to a beautiful woman's long full head of hair.

IT WAS SIMPLY BEAUTIFUL!

I could feel the dark cloud that had been hovering over me instantly vanish. Living under constant tension was over. I could finally breathe deeply without the stress of what potential negativity could randomly fall into my lap daily. In other words, it was now all good.

Observing so many contrasts to my prior life in a mere ten minutes was breathtaking. The movers finally arrived and proceeded to unload all of our belongings. Before leaving, I pulled the lead mover into the back bedroom to give the crew a tip. He thanked me as he exited the door, turned around, shook my hand again, and said, "Thank you, you deserve all the good fortune you are receiving."

Those comments further validated the experience of the entire day as well as all the work I put in to make this moment possible.

As was the case when we moved into the Drew Hamilton Projects twenty years earlier, there wasn't any food in the new apartment. Therefore, fast food was the logical option. Our first night in the projects, I recall my mom sending my sisters to the KFC on 145th and Lenox Avenue for a bucket full of wings, rice, and biscuits. I thought to go to the local KFC simply for the sake of keeping the tradition alive. However, a voice in my head whispered, *"You know they deliver to your door in this neighborhood, don't you?"*

I chuckled to myself while shaking my head. I never experienced or witnessed a delivery man deliver food to an actual door in my old neighborhood. In fact, the delivery of food was off limits due to the high risk of the delivery man being

robbed. The best I could have hoped for in the past was to meet

him downstairs in the freezing cold, and even that option was

only offered by only one establishment. Deliveries to downstairs

were absolutely off-limits during the summer because there

were too many people hanging out front during warm weather.

This dynamic probably seems ridiculous to those who have never

resided in the Trap; however, it is absolutely accurate.

Memories of being denied food delivery services

prompted me to order food delivery. I specifically chose Chinese

food since this was the closest thing to a fine dining

establishment in my old neighborhood. It was imperative that I

feel the rush of actually ordering food and it being delivered

pleasantly in a timely fashion TO MY DOOR.

My youngest sister was scheduled to stop by after work,

so I placed an order for her as well. The Chinese food arrived

twenty minutes later and my sister soon thereafter. She too

needed a grace period to comprehend a Chinese delivery

person actually delivering food to your door without any commotion.

To mainstream America, food deliveries are a commonplace occurrence, but to us, this meant the world. It symbolized the shackles being removed from our lives. We were gradually beginning to enjoy the norms of mainstream society.

While eating her Chinese food, my sister joked that she felt like Sara Jessica Parker's character, Carrie, from *Sex in The City*. Carrie would often eat Chinese food in her New York City apartment. Yet even more realizations occurred from being able to receive our food in this fashion, it confirmed that logically no one is loitering in the lobby and some of the inconveniences of living in the Trap were erased forever.

We were now a part of the New York City romanticized on shows like the hit series *Sex in The City,* and the feeling was euphoric.

For the next few days, we settled in, as we gradually became accustomed to the sounds of birds chirping, pleasant breezes coming from the Hudson River and the other pleasantries of our new neighborhood. I had taken a few days off from work to ensure our transition into the neighborhood was a smooth one. On the first morning of my return to work, I happened to be running late and needed to take a yellow cab. Skeptical at first, I considered the train to be the best option. In the past, I was hesitant even to attempt hailing a yellow cab due to the discrimination many African American men faced from this task, but since I now no longer perceived myself an outsider, I figured I'd test it out to see if this was, in fact, the case.

I confidently strolled to the corner with all the swagger of George Jefferson, put my arm out and this time magically within one minute a yellow cab calmly glided in to pick me up versus the herkie jerky hesitant pick-ups I experienced so often in the past.

The cab driver pried for information and grew inquisitively friendly after confirming I lived in the neighborhood. Naturally, he questioned me as to what nationality I was, how long have I lived in the area, and what I did for a living. Once I explained that I worked in healthcare, he stated, "That is the quickest way to go from nobody to somebody."

Since New York City cab drivers have a wealth of knowledge acquired from picking up a vast variety of passengers from Wall Street bankers to the minimum wage workers of the city, his words were even further affirmation that yes, I was indeed now "somebody." In the past, in his eyes, I probably would have been considered just another African American hoodlum that may jump out without paying, but now since I resided in the New York City which "mattered" I seemed to "matter" also.

As we rode through Manhattan from the west side down to the eastside, I reveled in the hustle and bustle of the city. For so long, I was stagnant, wasting away hours and days standing on the corners of my old neighborhood. The rush I felt from now

being a part of the action was indescribable. Once I reached my

job, the cab driver wished me good luck, and I proceeded to pay

the fare plus tip.

This day was particularly filled with affirmations of my

current state of being. I was assigned to work in the Emergency

Room CT scanner. The day was pretty uneventful until about

3pm when a group of correction officers escorted one of the

inmates from the prison within the hospital to the CT

department. There was a brief pause as I was the only person in

the room. The officers weren't exactly sure if I was an assistant,

student, or the actual CT technologist who was supposed to be

operating the scanner that day. The hesitation on their part

wasn't due to a racial issue since all three correction officers

were African American. I recognized that it was a combination of

pride and confusion. I believe they were dealing with an emotion

of joy due to seeing a young African American male in a positive decision-making role. Their day to day interactions consisted of overseeing a prison full of young males who look just like me. Through their occupation, perhaps it became mentally programmed that most young African American males in New York City were destined for Rikers Island. They were astonished and proud to see I veered off the expected course and changed my destination.

During the brief pause, all these possibilities raced through my head. To quell the awkwardness. I introduced myself and asked if this was the patient I was expecting. The officers politely confirmed the information for me, and I proceeded with the patient's' exam. The exam took about thirty minutes to complete.

As I performed the exam, the officers stood behind me in the control room and observed. One of the officers asked me, "How long have you been doing this, and how many years did you go to school?"

I responded, "two years of school and two and a half years working here."

A few more minutes went by, and the financial question followed as I assumed it would.

Another officer asked, "How much could you make a year doing this?"

Before answering, I chuckled, grinned, and then replied, "Anywhere between $60K -$110K, depending on how much you choose to work."

All three of their faces lit up with disbelief as they simultaneously exclaimed, "You are only twenty-four years old making $110,000 a year?"

I replied, "Yeah, it's crazy, a dream come true."

The inquisition continued. They asked, "Where are you from?"

I assumed they expected me to say the Middle East, Caribbean, or Africa since a large portion of darker skinned nurses, doctors, and other medical support staff have immigrated to the United States from these regions of the world.

I wittingly replied quickly, "I'm from Drew Hamilton projects."

The astonishment grew larger since one of the officers was from Harlem as well. He was fully aware of the extreme obstacles, and pitfalls I had to navigate to be sitting there speaking to him performing these CT scans with no supervision. In essence, I was running the show and had carved out my own destiny.

The exam was now completed, the officers congratulated me and encouraged me, "Stay on the path you on. Don't let any of your friends from your hood throw you off!"

Coincidentally the inmate had overheard the conversation and proceeded to grant me his respect by stating, "Yo, I respect you. I don't see too many of us in the position you in. Keep doing your thing."

These kinds of interactions would continue to occur every few months over the next several years.

As the inmate and correctional officers exited the room, a feeling of euphoria rushed through my body as had frequently been occurring since my life experienced a kind of rebirth. While I did feel a sense of extreme confidence and importance, I also realized I wasn't a neurosurgeon or cardiologist. Why was I being treated as if I was some sort of prodigy?

There was a distinct contrast when Caucasians would assess whether I was the person who was indeed going to be performing the exam versus when African Americans would assess. Caucasians appeared to be surprised just as African Americans, however, they usually wouldn't inquire as to how I reached the position I was in. They also seemed less likely to treat me with prodigy status, perhaps because many of their parents were doctors and nurses. They weren't as impressed as African Americans.

These contrasts granted me a window as to how uninformed African Americans have been kept in regard to educational opportunities. Being a CT technologist was a dream come true for me, whereas for many Caucasians I've interacted with in the medical field, becoming anything else than a doctor was viewed as a complete failure.

It seemed both Caucasians and African Americans appreciated the position I was in, but the difference was African Americans viewed it as a tremendous feat versus Caucasians who viewed it as fairly good for an African American.

Just as the officers did, most African Americans understood the daunting task it required for me to be there. This was yet another dynamic that I had to become familiar with due to the rebirth, which was rapidly occurring in my life.

I pondered over this interaction for the rest of the day, wishing that it would one day become commonplace for young males from the *other side of the tracks* to achieve success.

Later the same week, my employer, NYU Medical Center, held their annual Christmas party. The party was held at the Warwick Hotel located around the corner from Rockefeller Center in midtown Manhattan. The attire was semi-formal, and I decided to wear a suit. I owned a few suits which were forced on me by my parents a few years earlier, but they definitely were not my style. I'd heard descriptions of the ambiance of these parties from my co-workers but having never been to a formal affair I didn't fully understand what to expect.

The event was filled with top-shelf liquor and waiters serving platters of hors d'oeuvres, including the most delicious jumbo shrimp. A co-worker I was close with, who was also born into the Trap, attended the party. When the waiters came by with the shrimp filled platters, we both looked at each other smiling and in unison stated, "What the hell are we doing here?"

The emotions from our years of struggling culminated at this moment. It was as if we really meant to ask each other, "Are we going to wake up one day from this dream?"

However, since we had come to appreciate the discipline and ingenuity which was required to escape the Trap, we realized it was indeed a dream, a dream come true. We shook hands, embraced, and declared, "We made it," with a toast of champagne.

We danced all night with beautiful, elegant women, the type of women I hadn't previously had access to. Their perfume, hair scent, and skin radiance were different-- in a good way.

Everything was now different. It was everything I had watched in Martin Scorsese films growing up except we weren't gangsters, we were free to relax and didn't have to look over our shoulders when the party was over. As these thoughts ran through my head, I took in one of my reflective deep breaths and whispered to myself, "I did it my way, the right way."

I couldn't help but channel Frank Sinatra, the voice who embodied a great night on the town in New York City. I'd heard it is human nature to be resistant to change, however as the night ended and I stood looking out onto 46th Street and 5th Avenue I couldn't help but look up at Rockefeller Center, thank the Lord and pray that this rebirth wouldn't cease any time soon.

Over the next few months, I continued to find myself in establishments I once assumed weren't for people who came from where I was from. My co-workers were constantly going out to bars and lounges to unwind from the stresses of the medical field. Most of the establishments were located on the east side of midtown and downtown Manhattan. Prior to my rebirth, I would only venture into these neighborhoods to go shopping for apparel, and even then, I couldn't help but feel somewhat out of place.

My self-esteem was slightly battered nearly every time I ventured into the more affluent areas. We were taught in school,

"All men are created equal," however, the stark reality was that I was clearly born into a world of inequity. I would frequently look up at the high rises and notice most of them were outfitted with balconies. I imagined what it would have been like to grow up with the ability to step out of my apartment, take in a breath of fresh air, and overlook the entire city at any moment I pleased. I realized this perk of being born affluent would have provided me a huge sense of wonder and freedom my old neighborhood had not.

One breezy summer night as I stood on the balcony of a lounge looking out onto the bustling party district of 2nd Avenue in midtown Manhattan, my dreams of one day standing out on my own balcony appeared so much closer to becoming a reality.

The alcohol was flowing, the music was live, the atmosphere fun-filled, and the ladies diverse. The same kinds of women who would have likely been suspicious while walking past me on the street or riding the train just a few years earlier were now freely dancing with me all night long. As my rebirth continued, it became obvious to me in America if you have green in your bank account, it instantly made you more important while slightly decreasing the fear of your skin color.

As these insecurities created by the invisible barriers of society were gradually being erased from my psyche, I began to feel an urge to continue to place myself in more places I previously deemed restricted to me. It was now time to acquire a passport primarily for recreation purposes but also to test the perceptions of black men outside of the United States.

Over the next several months, I began to reference back to some of the vacation destinations I'd heard in rap songs growing up. From songs describing drinking daquiris in the Jamaica to others which spoke of the white sand beaches of St. Thomas

Hearing their vivid depictions of Jamaica and St. Thomas eliminated the need to do a ton of research to determine which would be my first two destinations outside the U.S.

While rap music made where to go an easy choice, rap couldn't aid me in finding a group of my peers with whom to travel. Sadly, for as many drug dealers and flashy dressers I'd known growing up, there was not a single person I grew up with who had the desire or financial means to travel anywhere outside the U.S. for even a few days. There were many people who always claimed to be "gettin' money," but during this period, they were nowhere to be found.

My close friend was three years into a five-year prison sentence, and during my period of being hell-bent on escaping the Trap, I'd allowed distance to grow between me and some of my other childhood friends. The inspiration rap songs gave me about traveling was marred by this cold hard fact.

As my so-called rebirth was rapidly occurring, I never stopped to consider that I wouldn't have many friends to enjoy my new-found success with unless I paid all the expenses.

In order to remove this feeling of isolation, I considered footing the bill for a group vacation, however, after a few weeks of contemplating, my street instincts led me in the opposite direction.

In the Trap, a simple act of treating your friends to a taste of luxury had to be brainstormed. Decisions, even those which emerged from the best places of your heart, could lead to your demise down the line. Paying for even two of my friends to travel out of the country would have sparked a frenzy of rumors in regards to my financial status which in turn could have possibly attracted all sorts of negative attention which could have initiated a robbery attempt or me killing someone in self-defense.

After wracking my brain for a few weeks, I chose Jamaica as the first place I would go. I nearly settled on St. Thomas, however the vivid description of the white sand beaches made me certain I needed to bring a beautiful woman along to genuinely enjoy the experience. Therefore, I ventured to Jamaica alone. After all, growing up in New York City, Jamaican culture and food was second nature to me. Some of my friends were Jamaican, and when I would travel to Brooklyn to visit my family, most residents had ties to the Caribbean. It just seemed organic that Jamaica should be the first place I venture out to.

The flight from New York City to Jamaica was about four hours. The airplane was filled with couples and groups of friends ready to enjoy all Jamaica had to offer. I was excited and didn't really think much about the fact I was on vacation by myself, although those thoughts would arise later when I actually arrived.

Upon my arrival, I decided to take a shuttle van for the two-hour ride from Montego Bay to Negril. The sun was beginning to set. I stared awestruck by the beautiful scenery for the whole ride. The countryside was filled with lush green land and rolling hills, the sun was gorgeous amber, and the air was the freshest I'd breathed thus far in my life. I had envisioned what Africa would look like, and for me, Jamaica was the closest thing since it was the first country, I'd visited whose population mostly derived from African descendants.

It was as if I was returning to my homeland.

As we entered deeper into Jamaica, I began to absorb the details of the architecture, the way people dressed, and their overall demeanor. Although it was immediately obvious Jamaicans had less economically than even some of the poorest African Americans in the U.S., the people appeared happier than many people in America of all races. I somewhat expected the opposite demeanor to be present since I'd grown up believing poverty is what causes you to walk around with a frown.

Upon my arrival at the hotel, I was greeted warmly and escorted to my room. It was about 9pm Jamaica time, since I was exhausted from the flight, I decided to rest in order to be fully prepared to enjoy the remainder of the trip.

Early the next morning, I headed out for my all-inclusive breakfast, followed by a little relaxation on the beach. After a few hours of lounging in my beach chair, I observed a young man about the same age as me walking up and down the beach selling trinkets. He was sweating tremendously from making numerous trips up and down the beach. As I observed him putting forth his best efforts to sell his goods, I began to reminisce on a time when a sudden thunderstorm came through New York City during rush hour. My brother was on bustling 125th Street as commuters ran under bus stops and store canopies for cover. Incredibly, he was able to buy a dozen umbrellas for the retail price then instantly resell all the umbrellas for thirty percent over retail within five minutes.

As I compared my brother's experience with that of the young man walking along the beach, I again realized that in many major cities in America much of the darker skinned population in urban areas had been led to believe we were poor when in fact it was merely a wealth disparity. The Jamaican young man didn't have the option to offer his goods to a thousand people walking down the street nor the option to ride the train as a street performer to generate income as is afforded to those who live in major urban centers of the U.S. In America, my brother made more money selling umbrellas within fifteen minutes in the pouring rain than the young man in Jamaica possibly could make in a week in the beautiful sunshine.

This glaring reality pushed me to befriend the young man in order to see what being born into the Trap in Jamaica meant for him. As he was walking past me yet again, I approached as if I was interested in buying a trinket. I assume he recognized I was there alone and similar in age to him. Even though I didn't buy a trinket, he offered to take me on a boat ride around the island since it was his other job. I was dumbfounded that he had the energy to have a second job. This solidified my intrigue, and I took him up on his offer.

The next day I met him and his friend/co-worker on the beach around noon. We headed out in their small boat for a tour of the island. It turned out I was the only person on the boat since I was being given a personal tour which I didn't realize when I accepted his offer the day before. My instincts honed in the Trap initially gave me a reason for pause. After all, there was a chance I could be kidnapped or even killed by going on an unauthorized tour with two strangers. I can remember an era in New York City when you constantly would get into a staring match with any African American or Latino your age who sat or stood directly across from you on the train. It was a duel to see who would turn or put their head down first. Being born into the Trap conditioned us to be overly cautious of young men who looked and acted just like us.

We needed to be certain you weren't a threat or even remotely interested in a confrontation. Bowing or turning your head served as confirmation of this. It was akin to being afraid of your own shadow, and although it seemed ridiculous, it was very much our reality. However, in this instance, rather than being fearful of each other, we seemed to bond instantly. He didn't appear afraid of me not paying for the tour, and I wasn't afraid of them robbing or hurting me. I could sense we saw each other as brethren. Yet again, I couldn't help but think about the possibilities if the camaraderie between young African American men were the same back in the U.S.

As we headed out into the ocean, we traded stories about our upbringings. We quickly noticed there were many similarities. He described how his mom worked extremely hard cleaning hotels as my mom did also. As I described my life in the U.S., he sat in awe of the things I'd experienced and the opportunities available to me. Despite how so many more opportunities were afforded to me, it was perplexing to me how we both grew up feeling as if we were doomed to a lifetime in the Trap, bar it some miracle happening. His plan to escape his Trap was to invent something that could be used by the entire world. A few years earlier, I attempted to invent a walker for babies that ended up not becoming a worldwide phenomenon as I assumed it naturally would. This similarity brought me back to the mind state prevalent in many traps that the only way to escape was through extraordinary accomplishments. It was the mental state I previously had, but as I sat on this boat with my new friend, I realized it were simple steps that allowed my initial escape from the Trap. Dreaming big is absolutely necessary especially when starting from the bottom depths of society, however, always betting on the long shot is a losing formula. In essence, neither my basketball dreams nor my invention had taken me to all the new places I once deemed weren't meant for kids like myself. Instead, it was a small decision to go to school for two more years, which had changed my life forever. Imagine if I had made the decision of either going to the NBA or inventing my walker and if those things don't work out, I'm just not going to try anything else. I probably wouldn't be sitting here having this conversation overlooking the ocean in Negril, Jamaica.

We continued to talk about the stresses of growing up in poverty, and we discussed how even though these conditions drained much of our innocence we were still able to see the beauty of life despite all the things we struggled with on a daily basis. This moment was truly a life-changing experience for me. As we stood upon the rocks looking out at the ocean, this portion of the conversation caused me to reflect on all the many good days I had while residing in the Trap. As the ocean breeze blew by, I stood still and thought about my ancestors who resided in slave quarters, which I compare to modern day housing projects. Despite these substandard living conditions, somehow, African people have never lost the ability to smile, dance, and create some of the most beautiful things humanity has ever known. At this moment, it became apparent to me it was ingrained in my DNA to become who I was truly meant to be despite having resided in the belly of the beast.

I arrived in Jamaica questioning how I survived long enough to see this moment, however after this conversation I was certain I would leave Jamaica no longer feeling *lucky* but instead now knowing it had been destined for me to carry on my ancestors' tradition of overcoming enormous obstacles all along. I was eager to return to America, so I could walk with my head even higher and feel even more comfortable in the places I once believed I didn't belong.

After the boat tour around the island, we returned to the beach, where he offered to join me at a nightclub. Later that night my new friend Kevin escorted me to the *jungle*, a well known nightclub in Negril located directly across from the resort I was staying at. We met out front at the designated time we agreed upon. I expected him to bring a few more people along, but surprisingly, he came alone. There was a small chance he maybe had people already waiting inside, however by this time his demeanor came across totally benevolent. Despite his gentle nature, the mentality of the Trap had been so ingrained in my soul I couldn't refrain from questioning whether this guy was befriending me in order to set me up for a robbery. My Trap view

of the world couldn't have been further from the truth. All he
wanted was to drink a few beers and party with the beautiful
ladies. After I bought him his first beer, I could see in his eyes he
was having a great time and eventually midway through the
night the fears running through my head vanished. The night
flew by as we danced with local Jamaican women as well as
international tourists. I felt incredibly blessed and of high
importance at the end of the night.

He treated me like family and even introduced me to a beautiful
Jamaican local who resembled *Downtown Julie Brown*, the MTV
VJ from the late '80s and early '90s whom I'd had a crush on as a
child. The two of us planned to hang out the next day. It was as if
I was DMX in the classic hip hop movie Belly, receiving a red-
carpet tour of Jamaica. One of the best nights of my life thus far
ended uneventfully, and I returned to my hotel room.

I occupied most of the next day with my Jamaican female
friend who I met at the Jungle nightclub the night before. I
instructed her to meet me in the lobby at noon, and she arrived

promptly. She wore a beautiful sundress and her hair was styled in gorgeous long braids with brown highlights. In my eyes, she represented exactly what I imagined a native Jamaican woman would look like. It was once again a gorgeous breezy, sunny day as we headed into town so I could experience the true culture of Negril. We spent most of the day riding around Negril visiting local strip malls and tasting the authentic local cuisine. As we moved around Negril, my Trap mentality briefly resurfaced as I pondered if this beautiful woman was really a decoy planning my demise. Here I was in Negril maneuvering throughout the city with this gorgeous woman, whereas throughout most of my youth I couldn't even travel to an unfamiliar neighborhood let alone another city without genuine concern for my safety. I'd heard many stories from Jamaicans who resided in Brooklyn about the violence in Kingston, Jamaica, however, regarding Negril there seemed to be an affinity between brown people which I hadn't had the luxury of experiencing thus far. As the sun set, we headed back to my resort and had to part ways since the locals were forbidden from entering. We exchanged a warm embrace as she whispered in my ear, "I have to see you one more time before you leave."

These words resonated with me throughout the remainder of my trip. She didn't have a home phone, and I had previously scheduled excursions for the next few days; therefore, the odds of this moment being our last encounter were high. Over the next four days, a majority of my mental capacity was occupied, hoping I would be reunited with her on the beach.

Just as I was beginning to become despondent about never seeing the Jamaican Queen again, I noticed another beautiful tanned woman whose curly brown hair flowed more than halfway down her back walking in the opposite direction. At first glance, I couldn't believe my eyes. It was as if I was witnessing a real-life mermaid. As we neared each other, her beauty was even more stunning, and my heart began racing. However, the closer I got a sense of peace came over me. We instantly made eye contact. I couldn't help but wonder if she was having the same thoughts about me. It seemed as if time stood still and then when we were finally parallel, she cracked a smile, and I said, "Hello, how are you?"

She replied, "I am well," as we gazed into each other's eyes. I asked her if she was here alone and she inquired also. We both confirmed we were indeed alone and proceeded to take a long walk down the beach, growing increasingly comfortable with each passing moment. She stated she was an Iranian national who was a teacher in California. In my eyes, her being Middle Eastern added a mystique to this entire encounter. My world was once again becoming bigger, and the previous confinements were yet again being removed. She had no idea I was a kid from the projects in New York City and wouldn't have believed me even if I told her. It also didn't matter that I was twenty-three years old and she was forty-one. We were simply in awe of each other as we continued our stroll down the beach. The sunshine soon turned into clouds, and a thunderstorm soon followed. By this time, we were so far away from our hotel rooms, we decided to swim in the ocean. It was euphoric, the rain was cold, but the water was warm, thus giving my senses the perfect balance needed for this occasion. As we swam in the Jamaican waters, she gracefully swam away from me appearing and disappearing just as a mermaid would. Even at this juncture, I didn't rule out that she may just disappear into the abyss, and my fantasy would come to an end. Then just as I was having this thought, she reappeared and proceeded to hug and kiss me passionately. Our encounter was electric, and soon thereafter, the thunder roared louder, and flashes of lightning blazed across the sky. We braved the weather conditions as long as we could, determined to make the electricity between us last forever. As the flashes of lightning increased, we were ordered out of the water by the beach security and lifeguards.

When we exited the ocean, the rain was still pouring down. Her long beautiful hair sparkled as if she moisturized her entire mane. Her two-piece bikini became slightly see-through as her skin, and toned body glistened from the rain. We found shelter under a canopy for a brief moment in the hopes the rain would subside. As we looked into each other's eyes, it was obvious the attraction was mutual, and she repeatedly stated such. After about fifteen minutes of conversation, the rain hadn't even minimally subsided, causing us to head toward my hotel room, which was closer than hers. Under normal circumstances, visitors were not allowed on the premises; however, due to the torrential downpours, all the security guards had taken cover and were nowhere to be found. My new friend requested to take a shower in my hotel since hers was so far away. I began to feel as if I'd hit the lottery since all the signs appeared to be pointing towards me living the American dream. She proceeded to invite me to join her in the shower. As the warm water ran down our bodies, we kissed passionately as we caressed.

This was the most beautiful woman I'd been intimate with up until this point. We cuddled for a few hours after making love when she returned to her hotel room shortly after the rain stopped.

This experience transformed me into a new man, the world seemed limitless, and I couldn't wait to return home so I could show off photos of this beautiful woman I had the pleasure of spending time with.

As this magical encounter temporarily faded into the distance of my mind, I couldn't help but wonder what happened to *Downtown Julie Brown*. Although the experience with the beautiful Iranian was splendid, something inside of me needed to experience the true essence of a Jamaican woman. I needed to learn about her life's triumphs and struggles. I wanted to know if the legend of the native Jamaican woman were true. I spent my final three days walking on the beach and in surrounding neighborhoods in the hopes of becoming reunited with her. On the second to last day, as I was relaxing on the beach, I couldn't believe that Rachelle's 5'8", 135-pound frame was actually walking towards me wearing a tank top and daisy duke styled jean shorts that accentuated her gorgeous Jamaican figure. Her beautiful braids had just been redone, and the sun glistened from her bronze skin and pretty white teeth. Her nails were painted a bright red. Even without access to the top of the line fashions and makeup products, she was no less stunning than any woman in the U.S. It was quite a remarkable sight, and her personality was equally beautiful. As she approached me in all her glory, she stated, "I been looking for you! Are you happy to see me?"

Naturally, I replied, "Of course, I am."

We remained on the beach for an hour then proceeded to walk down Norman Manley Boulevard until the sunset. She shared stories of daily life in Jamaica, and I reciprocated about growing up in a rough environment and how my life had changed so dramatically for the better. The story which was most profound to me was her describing if a woman is a victim of domestic violence in Negril, there would be no avenues to seek justice or protection unless you were wealthy. This dynamic yet again magnified the fact in many ways despite being born into the Trap in America, I was far better off than many others throughout the world.

After hours of deep conversation, the physical attraction became far greater. Rachelle expressed her desire to spend the night together. Since she was fully aware the resort wouldn't allow her to enter, she directed me to a local hotel on the cliffside, which would be convenient. As we lay in bed watching TV for almost two hours, she pulled a book of matches from her bra, lit the red candles in the room, and began rubbing my face while kissing my lips. I slowly undressed her as I marveled at her goddess-like physique. While my experience with the beautiful Iranian woman was ultra-sensual, this rendezvous was everything all in one package.

As I woke up the next morning, while staring at this statuesque bronze woman lying next to me,

I whispered to myself, "Wow, the legend of native Jamaican women is real."

In my wildest dreams, I couldn't have imagined these experiences just a few years earlier. However, by God's grace and much effort on my part, my rebirth appeared to be completed with me virtually unscathed. Later that afternoon as I headed to the airport once again traveling along the countryside from Negril to Montego Bay, I spent the entire ride reflecting on how this vacation forever transformed me and how my life would continue to expand upon my return to New York City.

Life After Freedom

The taste of freedom after escaping the Trap was bittersweet. I celebrated and rejoiced in my freedom, yet I felt sharp pangs of sadness and remorse for all the others I'd left behind. Even the grandest of vacations or luxury vehicles couldn't suppress the dichotomy I constantly faced. If I chose to revel in the freedom of my success, I would be considered a sellout, a traitor to the neighborhood I grew up in. The guilt was gut-wrenching.

Is this how the slaves who escaped to freedom on the Underground Railroad felt?

Did they feel guilty for enjoying freedom while their friends and family members remained trapped on the plantation?

No matter how much I tried to wean myself from the effects of my old neighborhood, my deep emotional turmoil caused me to be susceptible to making poor choices and decisions based on my guilt. Even the new relationships I entered were affected.

The first example of this was when I began dating a fairly well-known neighborhood girl. Although she was five years my senior, I was captivated by her 5'9", 160-pound frame—she reminded me of supermodel Naomi Campbell. Despite our intense chemistry, we had very few things in common.

I was now an ambitious twenty-five-year-old professional, earning $100,000 a year, with aspirations for even more.

She was a thirty-year-old single mother receiving government assistance, with a twelve-year-old daughter who unfortunately became pregnant during our relationship.

Most of my family members strongly disapproved of our relationship, however, I was unable to separate myself from her due to my fear of appearing to have acquired a new-found superiority complex— or as we called it in the Trap, acting "brand new." In other words, I wanted to "keep it real."

I had mostly conquered my attachment to the dysfunctional parts of the trap but continued to struggle with letting go of this dysfunctional relationship. Subconsciously, I was determined to elevate her standard of living despite all the resistance I was met with from both her and the Universe.

I recall her daughter running away from her suburban New Jersey home to her aunt's apartment in the notorious River Park Towers in the South Bronx to be closer to her slightly older boyfriend. During this time, alleged incidents of domestic violence between the two young teens prompted me to accompany my girlfriend on numerous missions to go looking for her daughter. During one of these missions into the River Park Towers, it was alleged her daughter's boyfriend and his friends were planning on attacking me for coming to defend her. Although I was accustomed to this type of conflict due to my 20 years of residing in the projects, this was the exact type of thing I worked so hard to escape. By God's grace, the young boys chose not to act on their plans, which would have certainly required retaliation on my part. Ironically, this situation served to magnify the fact I was at a crossroads between forever escaping the Trap and being pulled back in without a second chance to escape.

Nonetheless, I persisted by attempting to expose my girlfriend to a more peaceful existence which life now afforded me—something she had never experienced before our relationship. I honestly believed treating her to the finest restaurants and taking her on vacations would somehow cause her to see possibilities of life without turmoil. Yet, the harder I tried; the more chaos arose.

My biggest reward for escaping the Trap was traveling. After being restricted for so long, I was excited to have the freedom to see the world. Since she was my girlfriend, I figured I would reward her as well by exposing her a different form of living. On a trip to Barbados, we dined at the finest restaurant on the island. The food was tremendous, and the ambiance was spectacular. We sat at a table adjacent to the ocean with the waves splashing on the rocks as we dined. While I was certainly focused on the awesome ocean view, I also couldn't ignore the fact we were two of only four people of the darker hue out of over two hundred patrons of the establishment.

The bittersweet feelings of escaping the trap surfaced yet again.

I'd known individuals who never traveled outside of Harlem, nonetheless to a five-star restaurant in Barbados. Many were resistant to venturing out due to fears of not being accepted in the so-called high-end areas. My girlfriend suffered from the same mentality. The more I attempted to elevate her life and expose her to new things, the more she resisted. Her daughter and sister despised me and began to accuse her of acting bougie, which in turn led to almost weekly conflicts which could have escalated to violence. I was exposing myself to unnecessary risk, which could forever keep me in the Trap due to attempting to maintain some false credibility. I came to a crossroad where I had to decide whether I wanted to continue traveling the world and eating at the finest restaurants or holding on to the false notion of "keeping it real "with people and situations which would ruin my life. My decision to separate myself from anything which could cause me to remain stuck in the trap caused some of my closest friends to label me as bougie and even some family members labeled my new healthy eating habits as eating like a "white person."

Eventually, I decided even if I began to be viewed as not "keeping it real", a life of leisure spent traveling the world and eating at the finest restaurants was better suited for me than the life of dysfunction filled with constant tension and flare-ups of violence. I spent twenty years living under this constant tension. I realized I now deserved to completely let go and live the life we all should be destined to have. As a result, I parted ways with my girlfriend and anyone else who wasn't able to free themselves from the addiction to the stresses of the Trap.

Once I freed myself from the guilt of escaping the Trap, the floodgates of my new life opened. The vacations continued. I purchased my first car and my first home at the age of twenty-five. I'd previously heard the phrase "it's lonely at the top," and the more successful I became, the fewer people I had to enjoy it with. At this point I was now living in Midtown Manhattan and rarely ventured to my old neighborhood.

Having previously heard all the wild stories of Spring Break, I recall eagerly having hopes of taking a group vacation to Cancun, Mexico. During the early phases of planning, I quickly realized I was no longer in contact with many of my childhood friends and the others either couldn't afford to go or lacked the desire to travel. Nonetheless, I proceeded to venture out on my own to the Riviera Maya area of Cancun, Mexico. The vacation was flawless despite the lack of company, and I had several epiphanies about how my success and status affected the way others view me.

The most memorable portion of the trip was during a catamaran tour through the Yucatan Peninsula. Once again, I was the only darker skinned person on the excursion. The captain of the catamaran was a native Mexican with a great deal of knowledge about the world. He programmed the latest music and steered the catamaran over the crystal blue waters at what I assume was the maximum speed limit. The captain and I discussed our love for Range Rovers, shared pictures of the ones we owned as well as his private plane. The next natural occurrence was for him to ask, "So, what do you do?"

I proceeded to say radiology. The word was barely out of my mouth when the beautiful photographer who worked on the catamaran said, in her Mexican accent, "you're a doctor?"

Before I could clarify my actual occupation, the photographer was inquiring how long I would be in Cancun and what hotel I was staying at, thinly disguised as an attempt at being accommodating by offering to personally courier my photos directly to my resort. After the splendid five-hour tour of the Yucatan Peninsula which was spent eating fresh lobster and drinking rum punch, we returned to the boat docks with plans of seeing each other on at least one more occasion. A few days later, she arrived at my hotel room in a royal blue bikini and my tour photos in hand. Although there was a slight language barrier, our eyes spoke the same language fluently. I couldn't help but wonder whether it was indeed our eyes or my perceived financial status, which so rapidly eroded the cultural barrier.

The intoxication of freedom and success caused me to continue to push the envelope and continue working hard to experiment just how many barriers my new-found freedom could eliminate. I continued to dine at fancy restaurants throughout different cities across the United States and islands throughout the Caribbean, waiting for the day I would be treated less than favorably. I must have patronized at least forty high-end restaurants, and not once was I viewed as not being able to afford the bill or anything discriminatory. Perhaps it was due to the confidence I carried from knowing I was more than equipped to pay for even the most expensive cuisine.

Even though I was aware of the financial disparity between African Americans and Caucasians and having been taught America is practically the only country in which you can

change the economic status you were born into, I still didn't want

to believe I would be given preferential treatment due to my

new financial status. I was idealistic in a sense. I strongly believe

everyone should be treated with the same respect regardless of

economic status.

However, the reality was far different than my fantasy.

Another byproduct of success (which was a form of

preferential treatment) was the new-found ability to date

beautiful women of other races. Prior to achieving success, a

woman outside of my race never wanted to date me. I previously

learned of this phenomenon regarding athletes and entertainers,

but I didn't realize it applied to regular six-figure earners as well.

In fact, dating was the tip of the iceberg. I became seriously

involved with three different women of other races in the first

eight years of my new financial status, two of which wanted to

be married and I casually dated many more.

The first experience I had with my new-found dating freedom was during the first year of my education in the radiology program. The most attractive woman in a class of about twenty-five students was a thirty-year-old curly haired blonde Lebanese who stood about 5'6". She was a fit 125 pounds due to her healthy obsession with her Stairmaster. During our first week of school, I certainly noticed her attractiveness though I couldn't perceive she would be interested in me. During week two, her eyes let me know she was highly interested in me, and her words followed soon after. Although she was eight years my senior, the relationship quickly grew intense. Practically every day after school, we would ride the train to her apartment in the predominantly Russian and Jewish Brooklyn neighborhood of Borough Park. While in school, traveling the New York City subway system, and walking through her neighborhood, I was amazed no one ever blinked an eye regarding our relationship despite our vastly different backgrounds.

She was very intrigued by my upbringing in the housing projects of Harlem. She was blessed to be from a privileged background and wondered how I managed to overcome my circumstances and make it into the radiology program. This was the center of her attraction, my ability to overcome the Trap represented a symbol of strength. Our attraction was irresistible, so irresistible that one month into our liaison, she notified me of her 8-year relationship with her boyfriend who was paying for her tuition and apartment. Despite learning this information, we grew more inseparable, and eventually, her boyfriend/benefactor became aware of our relationship. In a twist of irony, although we encountered zero discrimination from outsiders, the first incident of such occurred during a heated conversation in which he called me to demand we cease our relationship.

After trading insults, he proceeded to inform me that she couldn't possibly want me because "I was black and poor."

In another twist of irony, my girlfriend/lover found an ATM receipt which I accidentally left on her bed a week before which showed an account balance of approximately $18000 all of which was earned legally. On the other hand, however, I previously learned her boyfriend was, in fact, a drug dealer, and although I lived in the projects, I was in a better financial position than him. She proceeded to reassure me I was more of a man than her boyfriend in every way. I basked in the irony of the so-called underprivileged "POOR BLACK" kid from the projects attracting the privileged girl and being called black and poor by the Caucasian/Hispanic drug dealer who also grew up privileged. He assumed I was poor because of my skin color and where I lived. This irony served to prove what I believed to be true since I was eight years old. All white people weren't better off financially than blacks. The main difference appeared to be most blacks were born into a real trap, and most whites were born into real freedom. This was yet another indication I was at the cusp of finding true freedom and forever escaping the Trap. It also reinforced my ideology that being born into the Trap can be a blessing in disguise if you can navigate it correctly.

 As my journey through life after freedom continued a strange dynamic began to take hold of my personal life. It became increasingly difficult to attract African American women. In an eerie twist of irony, other races grew more attracted to me while African American women began to reject me often stating I was too bougie for their taste. This new trend left me both perplexed and saddened, causing me to attempt resisting it at all costs.

Despite all my efforts to date within my race, the interracial trend showed no signs of ceasing. During this time, I moved from New York City to Atlanta, Georgia, which has long been known as the mecca in the United States for African American symbols of success. Atlanta is also located in the state of Georgia whose state flag once included the hateful Confederate symbol which I liken to a swastika. These two contrasts symbolized the dynamic I was about to encounter in my new relationship with a country girl born in a rural town deep

in South Georgia.

I was familiar with stories of guys from the ghetto going

to college and being introduced to dating outside their race, so I

came to view dating my college classmate a few years prior as

commonplace. Dating my college classmate was one thing;

however, dating a voluptuous corporate blonde, blue-eyed

medical sales representative who earned over $150,000 per year

was another. This isn't to say dating another race is something to

aspire to, it simply was something which just a few years prior

was basically out of the realm of possibility. We simply had no

prior means of ever crossing paths, but our education bridged

the gap.

On a sunny afternoon in the spring, as I sat in front of my

CAT Scan machine awaiting the representative to arrive, I could

hear her high heels as she traveled down the hallway. I was

pleasantly surprised at who would be training me on my new

medical device, and she too appeared pleasantly surprised as to who she would be training.

The young man born into the projects in Harlem and the country girl born the backwoods of Georgia who admittedly has racist parents, bonded instantly. We discussed healthcare, politics, and race for hours. The energy was so magnetic I could see her turning red as we agreed on various topics regarding the many false notions we were taught from our respective cultures. Within weeks we began dating, eating out at the high-end restaurants in Atlanta, meeting up in various cities throughout the U.S., and taking vacations. Throughout our time together, we never encountered a racist incident; however, I would notice glances, which suggested she might be financing our rendezvous. Perhaps her corporate look coupled with her blonde hair and blue eyes automatically registered as affluence to some people or maybe they too assumed I was black and poor. Thankfully, this couldn't be further from the truth. In fact, due to her student loans and other factors, I was far more

financially stable despite having been born into the Trap.

Once again, the perception of every single Caucasian

being more financially well off than every black person proved to

be false. Perhaps her grandparents were more well off than my

parents, but I certainly had bridged the wealth gap we were

born with. On paper, we were compatible, both attractive six-

figure earners who had no children. However, as our

relationship became more serious, and we discussed her racist

parents, I couldn't foresee subjecting a child of mine to name

calling and inferior treatment. We parted ways and remained

friends.

I continued dating, now exclusively searching for an

African American woman, and there were plenty of them at

Grady Memorial Hospital where I worked. From nurses to

aspiring doctors, this was probably the largest pool of attractive,

educated, and successful African American women I would ever have daily access to. About a year into my employment, I began dating a nurse who was the epitome of an African American goddess. Her skin was like caramel silk, and she adorned long braids. If I woke up in Africa to my dream girl, she would have been the prototype.

We initially had great chemistry, and on paper, we were a perfect match. I was under the impression she was the Nubian queen I yearned for therefore I pulled all the bells and whistles attempting to paint a picture of what life could be for us in the future. Since money was practically no object for me, we ate at fancy restaurants, planned on realizing bucket list vacations, and attended *Cirque du Soleil* shows as VIPs where we were allowed to meet the performers backstage. Unfortunately, although she was a Registered Nurse in the ICU at a major hospital in a major city, upon her first visit to my $400,000 townhouse she informed me that I was far more accomplished than her and suggested that a Caucasian corporate CEO who didn't already have her own children would be a perfect match for me. This interaction left me bewildered and in disbelief due to me always being told that success would automatically bring me the woman I always dreamed of. I was familiar with the phrase it's lonely at the top, but this experience magnified yet another negative side effect of becoming successful. It seemed my new-found financial success made it difficult to maintain relationships both with friends and the opposite sex.

As I continued to navigate my way toward my completion of what I deemed the *American Dream*, I decided to pursue a happy medium between the corporate Caucasian and the prototype African American woman. My instincts led me towards dating a woman with Latin heritage, however, being in Atlanta made this a slightly daunting task. In my opinion, there were thirty African American women for every Latina I came across. As luck would have it, in my community of $400,000 plus townhomes, my next-door neighbor appeared to be of Latin descent due to her tanned skin and light brown eyes. (Whether it was good or bad luck will become apparent later in this chapter.)

I would often see her passing by in her vehicle, but for months on end, we never had a chance to communicate until finally one day her mail was mistakenly placed in my mailbox. This was the opportunity I waited for, so naturally, I promptly strolled next door with the hopes she would answer. To my great pleasure, she did.

Her blue eyes lit up, and her tanned skin turned red from blushing. I proceeded to introduce myself and give her the package. We gradually became friends, and although many of our friends recommended we pursue a deeper relationship with one another, it took three years for us to finally begin dating. On paper, we appeared to be a match made in Heaven. We were both the same age, young homeowners, and successful in our own right. I was working in radiology while building my real estate business, and she was a Nurse Practitioner/ Nurse Midwife who acquired two master's degrees from a prestigious university in Atlanta. These factors, coupled with our friendship, aided in the relationship evolving rapidly.

Secretly, I incorrectly believed this relationship symbolized the epitome of success for a young African American man born into the Trap. Her parents were evangelical Christians from Northern California, and to my surprise, they embraced me with open arms. We couldn't have been any more opposites culturally; however, I believed my success was the main reason I was able to transcend these differences. I sort of felt like an athlete or entertainer whose success usually granted them access to all races and this was my first time being exposed to an affluent family. Her family was involved with the Foxy Lettuce Corporation and owned a winery in Monterey, California. Although there weren't many African Americans in Monterey, California, I was made aware she began dating African American men almost exclusively upon moving to Atlanta, Georgia. We often laughed at the fact her curvaceous figure, and tanned skin attracted more African American men, so therefore her choice in men was natural. This became her preference upon her move to the so-called African American mecca.

Yet again, I was thrown for a loop, and my preconceived notions were crushed. She was the least likely person I would have expected to date African Americans based on her background and cultural upbringing. If I thought this was the final time my preconceived notions were to be proven wrong, I was sorely mistaken.

A few months into our relationship, we ventured to Yuma, Arizona, for her brother's wedding. I was fully aware of Arizona's history of voting against the Martin Luther King Jr. Holiday so there was a bit of skepticism on my part. Also, I hadn't attended a wedding since I was six years old and while that wedding was lavish, this was on a completely different scale. It was an outdoor wedding with roughly five hundred guests, and I must emphasize, yet again, I found myself in a setting where I was one of the few African Americans. Not a single person other than me and a limousine driver were African American. Since I'd never been in an environment in which I was the sole African

American who was there by choice, I was slightly worried I might

be mistaken for a waiter or limousine driver. My worries couldn't

have been anymore baseless. Initially, I wondered if it was my

thousand-dollar suit, which buffered me from any prejudice;

however, I soon learned some of the attendees grew up farming

which in turn taught them great values and humility. Many of

them ascended to affluence, and although the wedding was

indeed extravagant, there was not a single ounce of arrogance

within the vicinity. I was just as comfortable at this wedding in

Yuma, Arizona, as I would have been at a wedding in Harlem,

New York.

Even with all the positive reinforcement, the wedding

experience provided me, I wondered slightly if the lack of any

racial undertones could be attributed to the fact we were in the

setting of a wedding where most people are usually in good

spirits. If I was uncertain, the Universe provided me with yet

another opportunity to remove my doubts once and for all.

My ex-fiancé's grandfather, who was a pillar in the community in Northern California met an untimely demise while on a golf outing. Due to his large influence on the community, he received a large funeral procession. For perspective's sake, imagine the five hundred attendees of the wedding in addition to another five hundred individuals gathered in a canyon in the hills of Salinas, California. The procession was huge and yet again, unlike anything I'd previously experienced. It was as if the Universe was telling me, "If you didn't believe five hundred white people can't be prejudiced, let me show you one thousand won't be either."

In addition to there being twice the amount of people, many of the men at the post funeral gathering were dressed down in farming attire and appeared far more rugged than those at the wedding. Based on their tattoos, many of them could have been bikers, and I sure knew biker gangs weren't necessarily African American friendly. My mind began racing as I looked around and absorbed the sheer amount of people by whom I was essentially surrounded. I looked to my black"

brotha" from another mother for comfort- the limousine driver

from the wedding. The presence of another African American

didn't stop me from briefly thinking what if these people decide

to turn on us. Images of photos of lynching's flashed into my

mind due to a large number of whites gathered in comparison

to blacks. These foolish thoughts subsided as I was introduced

to person after person who greeted me with all the grace and

respect, I could expect. The humility and respect were once

again displayed by the wealthiest man in the canyon who

tirelessly manned the grill for hours and served all the guests'

giant steaks and hamburgers.

On this day there was no thousand-dollar suit to shield

me from prejudice, and in fact, I didn't need it. By the end of the

night, I realized while racism does indeed exist, a majority of the

things African Americans and Caucasians have been taught

about race were unequivocally

false.

Basking, in my apparent freedom from the Trap, caused me to continue to push the envelope to confirm the degree of freedom I had attained. Throughout my life, I constantly heard various successful African Americans state that at some point, I would be reminded that America viewed me as a second-class citizen. However, thus far, I felt every bit as American as any White Anglo-Saxon Protestant. In fact, I viewed myself as having black privilege due to being able to escape the Trap. I was driving luxury cars without being pulled over by police, lived in neighborhoods where mail packages left on the porch for weeks weren't stolen, was able to go for a long run without fear of police officers mistaking me for a suspect, and had an overall sense of equity and freedom. In my eyes, how could anyone view me as inferior when I won at the game of life which was rigged against me?

I viewed myself as extraordinary. I had never been in prison or even been placed in handcuffs in my thirty-two years of life. Things were fantastic, and my ex-fiancé and I were enjoying the high life. There seemed to be no end in sight.

I can recall taking a lavish vacation to Turks and Caicos where I proposed by giving her a two and a half carat white gold diamond ring appraised at $25,000. We enjoyed a fancy dinner at the famed Anacaona resort. I was living a drug dealers' dream without having ever sold a drug in my life. In fact, I was living as well as, if not better than many rappers. The biggest difference was I was at less risk of being shot or needing an entourage of thirty guys with me for protection. While many celebrities were successful, it seemed they often paid a high price to obtain it. The feeling of true freedom was intoxicating due to the fact society appeared never to have expected me to be living this privileged life. Many of my peers mocked me for daring to believe I could acquire such a lifestyle.

During the period after I proposed to her, we traveled to Aruba, Dominican Republic, Cancun, and Cabo San Lucas not primarily for vacation but to scout the wedding venue. I can recall her, stating, "oh my God, we go on vacation to places where the average person dreams of having their honeymoon." Despite growing up privileged, even she was awestruck at the things I exposed her to.

Her statement once again put my life into perspective, and I felt truly vindicated.

Growing up in New York City, I would often dream of one day eating at a fancy restaurant on 5th Avenue. Upon a trip to the Big Apple, my dream materialized as we ate at a five-star restaurant on guess where? 5th Avenue.

As we exited the taxicab, I noticed an attractive New York City Police Department officer visually scanning me up and down as if she were attracted to me. Upon noticing my fiancé's two and a half carat engagement ring, the officer mumbled, "Oh, you must get money." When I heard her statement, I smirked.

As we entered the restaurant filled with mostly Caucasian patrons, we requested seating by the window. The courteous hostess obliged. We were seated next to a middle-aged Caucasian woman who would casually glance at us periodically. I thought to myself, "Here it is. This is the moment a racist is going to attempt to make me feel inferior."

I was wrong again.

The reality was she was enamored with the ring and commented on how lucky my now ex-fiancé was to have received such. By this point, I'd decided to give up on seeking the moment of truth in which race would play a factor in a common interaction.

A few months later I called off our engagement due to differences in temperament. We eventually battled in court over the engagement ring. To my dismay she tip toed on the edge of using the race card by telling the judge she was "afraid" of me, which is why she agreed to return the ring initially. After unsuccessfully attempting to regain the ring I continued to enjoy my unlimited freedom by enjoying Lamborghini excursions through the rocky mountains of Colorado, buying my first Rolex watch, and venturing to Dubai two times -even once enjoying the New Year's Eve fireworks display just underneath the colossal Burj Khalifa Tower which at the time was the tallest building in the world.

I was now living a life of true freedom, which was often more privileged than many people I encountered throughout my life who weren't *Born into The Trap.*

I must emphasize once again—I was able to obtain this freedom without ever having sold a single drug, becoming an athlete or entertainer, winning a lawsuit, or any other illegal activity. Thank God Almighty, I was free at last.

<u>Unscathed</u>

Escaping the Trap certainly wasn't easy.

There were many instances where my life could and should have taken a far different trajectory. Although I planned to escape since the first day I moved into the Trap, from the moment I decided to hang out in the streets, the Trap constantly sought to ensnare me forever.

Most of the instances in which I was nearly ensnared were due to my misguided actions. These misguided actions were partly due to the allure of the streets and the desire to mimic the gangster movies of the late 1980s and 1990s. I can recall seeing the commercial for the cult classic *King Of New York* which depicted gangster life in New York City. Up until this point, I cannot recall ever wanting to do anything besides enjoy being a child. Something about the raw imagery captured my attention. Realizing no one else would possibly allow an eight-year-old to see this movie, for weeks on end; I continually pleaded to my sister's seventeen-year-old boyfriend to make it happen. I could

sense he was like the characters in the movie, and he eventually

obliged to my wishes. Quite frankly, I became instantly

enamored with the ignorance and aggression of the gangsters

but was too young to realize these personas were only conducive

to the movies.

While leaving the movie theater, I can vividly recall a new-

found curiosity in taking on a tough guy persona. A figurative

battery had been placed in my back, giving me the boost needed

to maintain my aggressive behavior. It would take years of trial

and error for me to remove it. My elementary school comprised

of kids from the Frederick Douglass Housing Projects and mostly

middle-class kids. Upon returning to school, within a month, I

was ready to present my more aggressive persona, thereby

causing fights over the most minor incidents. Within a few

months, my toxic behavior began to spread to even some of the

middle-class children. Before long several of us were in a

competition to see who could have the most fights in every

school year. In retrospect, it is quite remarkable to think of the drastic metamorphosis within us. The previous school year, before implanting our tough guy demeanors, many of us endured the wrath of a bully almost every day. However, those days were a distant memory as I can recall us banding together to lure the former bully to a park to beat him with Billy clubs and hammers to exact revenge for his transgressions against us. It is important to emphasize we were around ten or eleven years old with these devious thoughts.

One afternoon we were minutes from carrying out our plan; however, the former bully seemed almost to smell the revenge within us, and fearfully declined to join us in the park. Even after we failed at luring him to the park, we continued to salivate at the idea of the former bully paying the price for his past disrespect. Soon after, the bully transferred to another school, and we were now satisfied that prior wrongs were made right. Thankfully, the universe preventing what would have been a horrific beating and our introduction to the prison system is one of many examples in which I narrowly avoided being forever ensnared in the Trap.

Although I recognized the severity of the horrendous act we nearly carried out, the saga continued as I tested how far I could take it until there would be ramifications for my actions. Nearly every day after school, we would seek out thrills in the form of starting trouble. Within the vicinity of our school were Riverside Park, Central Park, and The Frederick Douglass Housing Projects, which were usually our targets for seeking out our potential victims. Our mischievousness of choice was throwing rocks at joggers and construction workers, throwing items in the spokes of bikers' wheels, stealing from the local bodegas and concession stands, and strong-arm robberies of local kids. These acts would eventually lead to multiple incidents in which we were chased by civilians and police officers.

The first of these I can recall was when we decided to target a frankfurter concession stand run by an Eastern European gentleman, we nicknamed the "Frank Man." Two years before adopting our personas, we would patronize his business

uneventfully. However, the metamorphosis was now in full

effect, and it quickly became intoxicating to steal from this

hardworking gentleman. I vividly remember (with much shame

as I'm writing this) the first time we pulled off what was a grand

heist in our young minds. This grand caper netted us about three

dollars' worth of Cracker Jacks and juices. We were able to pull

off the scheme due to our unassuming nature. A friend of mine

picked up a box of Cracker Jacks and a few other items and asked

the gentleman, "How much is this?" The Frank Man replied,

"Fifty cents."

> playing coy, he replied, "Fifty cents? Fifty cents? Just the
> other day it was forty cents."

As he distracted the Frank Man, we proceeded to run

away with the items. I recall feeling a small sense of guilt by the

time I made it home that day. Yet, feeling one step closer to

being like the guys in *King Of New York* nullified any sense of

shame I felt. I believe since the seeds of mischief had been planted so deep within us, the only way our actions would cease was to be apprehended by law enforcement. Since we weren't caught the first time, we continued to harass the poor Frank Man practically every Friday, even recruiting new classmates who had become intrigued by the stories of our capers. Naturally, our numbers grew, and with every new attempt to steal from the Frank Man, the odds of someone calling the police grew as well. Eventually, a police chase ensued in which we had to run into the 96th Street and Central Park train station exiting at the 97th Street exit and escaping into a nearby apartment complex.

Even at this young age, we were clever enough to wait in the middle of the train platform to see from which entrance the police would come. By God's grace, they only pursued us via one exit; otherwise, we were prepared to risk our lives by running into the tunnels.

Undeterred, during this time due to engaging in so many misguided activities we never could predict when or where the next chase would occur. We were constantly seeking a new thrill.

The next thrill came in from some kids we had robbed two weeks

earlier whom we'd forgotten about.

On a sunny Saturday afternoon, as we were casually

roaming the Riverside Park area, we spotted our victims about

two blocks away walking in the park with their father, and

unfortunately, they spotted us too. Upon making eye contact, I

quickly saw the rage in his eyes from what his sons must have

detailed we did to them a few weeks prior. Recognizing they

would probably be calling the police, we immediately ran in the

opposite direction, but by the time we ran one block away, a

police car was in hot pursuit as we turned the corner. I

instinctively ran in a zigzag while my other friend ran in a straight

line and he was quickly apprehended. My friend was ordered to

enter a community service program, and even at the age of

twelve, he adhered to the code of not snitching by refusing to

implicate me and the others in the strong-arm robbery.

These two police chases were scary indeed, but they

didn't measure up to the time a group of my classmates and I were walking along Riverside Park as a male bicyclist and his

female companion rode by. As we would often do things without

warning for an increased thrill, my friend decided to throw a roll

of movie film he found on the ground in between the spokes of

the male's bicycle. This asinine act nearly caused him to tumble

over the front of his bike, and I could see him turn beet red and

the immediate rage in his eyes as he was in hot pursuit. We

instinctively ran in a circular pattern as it would be a difficult

maneuver for the bicycles to perform. Undeterred, the cyclist

hopped off the bicycle as we attempted to evade by running up a

grassy hill. Both parties filled with adrenaline now were in a

battle of wills of who wanted it more. The male cyclist snagged

one of my friends by the collar nearly capturing him, however,

my friend was able to contort his body in a supernatural fashion

releasing the hold the cyclist had on him. After what seemed like

an eternity, the forty-five-second pursuit ended due partly to

having youth on our side and the inability of the cyclist to

navigate the steep hill.

As I reflect on this terrible action on our part, I couldn't have blamed the gentleman if he would have chosen to injure or even kill one of us on this day. We certainly earned whatever justice he sought out. By God's grace, I was spared once again from the consequences of my actions.

By this time, I began to grow cognizant of the fact that I was extremely fortunate to have escaped the incidents unscathed thus far. However, I also gradually developed an invincibility complex. Being involved in multiple chases by the age of twelve still wasn't enough to cease my criminal activity. It was clear I was playing Russian Roulette with my future and grooming myself for a life of criminality. I began hanging out more in my Harlem neighborhood around 1991. Initially, all my peers and I did was play sports. By 1994, I'd lost contact with most of my junior high school friends. Around this same time, my neighborhood friends and I were engaging in the form of stealing called racking where twenty to thirty of us would go to various stores throughout the city and take as many items as possible.

Amid racking from time to time, we would also assault anyone who impeded our activity. For months, we didn't meet much resistance until one night in China Town when we encountered a merchant who wasn't going to allow us to terrorize him. Upon stealing about fifty items from his store, he proceeded to give chase apprehending one of my friends who was the only Caucasian residing in our entire housing projects.

This was the first time our loyalty to each other was put to the test as the merchant suspended his leg in the air as he lay on the ground after falling during the foot chase, threatening to break it in half via a thunderous kick. As we pondered whether to rush the merchant, he demanded we slowly roll back every item stolen from his establishment. Due to the distance between us, attacking the merchant would have been foolish as he would have snapped my friends' leg in half before we could reach him. By default, we obliged and slowly returned the items back to the merchant. He released our friend without injury and didn't appear to call the police.

Our young age and bravado caused my Harlem friends and me to continue to push the envelope just as my elementary school friends and I did. The illusion of the lack of consequences due to our age led most of us to believe there weren't any serious ramifications for our transgressions against others. This illusion, coupled with seeking the admiration of the older guys in our neighborhood, aided us in graduating from what was tantamount to shoplifting to armed robberies.

We noticed how their names were whispered with admiration throughout the neighborhood, and we sought to gain the same notoriety. When recruiting some of the younger guys to join their robbery crew, they would screen the candidates by asking, "Are y'all wolves or ballplayers?"

Many of us wanted to be known as wolves since there was a certain currency of such a title when you're born into the Trap.

In what seemed to be a never-ending pursuit to the bottom of society, to gain the validation of the older stick-up guys in the neighborhood and obtain wolf status, we now sought out to commit robberies by using firearms.

In my recollection, using a firearm during a robbery didn't net any additional proceeds versus strong-arm robberies not involving a gun. In both instances, we were approaching victims without having any idea whether the person was carrying fifty dollars or five thousand dollars. In most instances, the proceeds were less than five hundred dollars, split among five individuals. This reinforces the point that a firearm wasn't required to net a few hundred dollars from a robbery since we achieved this prior without using a gun. However, we wouldn't gain the validation of being a true wolf until we were brave enough, which is, in reality, foolish, to raise the stakes to the possibility of gunplay. It's amazing we never paused to consider the great risk we were undertaking versus the low rewards we received.

There are two incidents that provide concrete evidence of our foolishness and desire to seek validation from being labeled as stick up kids.

The first incident occurred on a winter afternoon as fifteen of us roamed the streets of Harlem looking for a victim while only one of us actually carried a gun. We descended on a check cashing place on 139th Street and 8th Avenue in Harlem, waiting for anyone who seemed like a viable target to exit the establishment. About twenty minutes passed without anyone exiting or entering, perhaps because they noticed a mob of young men lurking directly in front. As we grew impatient one of us noticed a police detective vehicle passing by heading downtown then reversing course by making a U-turn back in the uptown direction. As the detectives fast approached, the individual who carried the gun tossed it underneath a parked vehicle and simultaneously told me to pick it up to which I resisted. The detectives questioned why fifteen of us were lurking in front of a check cashing store in the middle of the afternoon. They searched all fifteen of us and upon not finding a weapon stated, "Don't make our job so easy."

It is my belief the officers knew exactly what we were doing but decided to be graceful and prevent our foolish demise. The officer's statement resonated with me, causing me to realize how ridiculous our actions were in addition to the meager profits a petty robbery would net amongst fifteen individuals. Most of us weren't in dire need of the funds. We were risking receiving ten or more years in prison solely to gain a reputation in our neighborhood.

Although we resided in the projects, many of our parents had decent paying jobs and provided us with the material things we wanted. In fact, about a third of my friends attended a catholic school. This incident marked the end of my partaking in any form of robbery as I realized the officer's words were factual. I finally understood for the past six years; I was essentially walking myself into captivity.

I was now awakened and began to shy away from my gangster desires. Despite this fact, simply continuing to linger in the neighborhood nearly tangled me in a web of a botched armed robbery in the Hamilton Heights section of Harlem.

On a cold winter night, I exited the back of my building headed down to my usual hangout on 142nd Street and 8th Avenue and within five minutes was notified of the botched robbery. My friends proceeded to tell me they attempted to rob a Jamaican man who resisted and began chasing them, causing one of them to drop the gun at the scene. Amazingly, the original participants were basically recruiting individuals to go back and retrieve the gun. I immediately recognized this would probably be a fatal mistake; however, my loyalty and peer pressure nearly caused me to foolishly return back up the hill with them to the scene of the crime. As I contemplated my next move, a feeling came over me, which led me to visit a friend of mine who lived in the Lionel Hampton Houses, one of the nicest high-rise buildings in Harlem. This was a preferred hangout of ours during the winter due to the beautiful twenty third floor views of New York City and nice furnishings.

Although his mother was a New York Police Department detective and a devout member of the Fruit of Islam organization, my friend too was a part of our robbery crew and would eventually succumb to being incarcerated. It was ironic on this day; both of us weren't in the mood to partake in any negative activity. I remained at his residence for about two hours as we discussed how we planned to escape the Trap.

Upon returning to my block, I learned seven of my friends had indeed returned to retrieve the gun. Unfortunately, as I expected, the police and the victim were awaiting their arrival. I narrowly escaped this trap. Meanwhile, my friends all received two to five-year prison sentences from this incident, which netted them zero dollars.

As the arrests mounted and my friends continued to disappear then reappear from stints in prison, I decided it would be wise to make a temporary escape from the Trap. My best

friend at the time had relatives residing in Savannah, Georgia.

After barely graduating high school, I planned on living

with him for the spring with plans of attending Spring Break in

Daytona Beach, Florida. This marked my first time outside of

New York City for an extended period of time and served as the

first glimpse of what life could be when I finally escaped the

Trap.

Upon my arrival, I could feel an instant connection to my

ancestors who were trapped on the plantations during slavery.

The air was clean, the demeanor of the people cordial, and the

large plantation homes were immaculate. In addition, there were

more symbols of African American success than I'd previously

witnessed. I had the opportunity to visit college campuses,

where ninety percent of the students were African American. Up

until this juncture I didn't realize predominantly African

American Universities existed.

During this trip, I grew fairly certain the traps which I previously laid for myself had disappeared forever since I began the process of minimizing detrimental behavior. However, being a young African American male born into the Trap meant even after removing self inflicted snares, there were still others lying in wait. The next potential trap didn't present itself until the end of the vacation as we attended Black Spring Break in Daytona Beach, Florida.

My dream of attending Spring Break events I watched for years on MTV had finally come to fruition. I was in awe of the sheer beauty of the women, beaches, and five-star hotels. I am forever indebted to my friend for granting me this experience afforded to very few guys in my neighborhood. In fact, this ignited the desire in me to travel the world. As it often happens at large events such as this, the warm weather and beautiful women weren't enough to stave off flare-ups of violence. Unfortunately, the flare-ups of violence we so desperately sought to avoid found us during a shootout between suspect and police, which resulted in me and three of my friends being shot, and the suspect killed.

As we enjoyed the festivities in front of the famed Adams Mark hotel amidst the one hundred thousand or so attendees, an individual who was not in my entourage slapped a female who rejected his advances. The female, in turn, notified an officer who quickly apprehended the suspect. The officer placed the suspect face down on the ground attempting to handcuff him. A large crowd quickly formed flinging bottles in the air and videotaping the arrest. As one the bottles hit the officer's shoulder, rolling down his arm, he grew increasingly uncomfortable with the large crowd which encircled him and reached for his gun. Having previously been a bystander in three shootouts, I recognized the need to immediately vacate the area. Within five seconds of attempting to walk away, a barrage of gunfire rang out and as I attempted to jump over a wall one of the bullets struck me in the left side of my back two inches from my spine. Feeling the sizzle in my back, which was akin to being burned with an iron, I began to panic as I pondered the extent of my injuries. The crowd dispersed, leaving me separated from my entourage. I began to walk the strip with my shirt raised over one arm to alleviate the hot sensation. I encountered a group of females driving and asked them to drive me down the strip to my hotel so I can reunite with my friends. Upon learning I suffered a gunshot wound, they immediately notified the first officer in sight. By this time, the incident was a top priority for the Daytona Beach Police Department and all the officers were on heightened alert. As I exited the females' vehicle on a dimly lit back street, the officer pointed his gun and flashlight towards me as I begged him not to shoot me. The officers slowly approached proceeding to frisk me for any weapons as I explained the events which led to my gunshot. I was placed in the back of an ambulance and since I had no exit wound, I was placed in the patrol car and taken to the police station for questioning.

My version of events was initially deemed suspicious due to the fact I had a hole in my back the size of the tip of my finger, however there was no hole in my shirt despite it being on when I was struck by the bullet. In what I deemed an attempt to see if I would change my story, I was interrogated for six hours by multiple police officers and detectives. Naturally, since neither my friends nor I had any connection to the incident, my story remained consistent. Understandably it was initially unfathomable to both the detectives and me that there wasn't a bullet hole in my shirt. By the end of six hours of interrogation, my shirt was taken to the forensics lab for testing. During the interrogation with the final detective, both he and I came to reason that only divine intervention could explain this unusual ballistic evidence. The trajectory of the bullet would have been directly in the line of my heart if it had exited via the front of my body. Perhaps I was graced, perhaps it was indeed divine intervention. I never received the forensics report from the Daytona Beach Police Department. Miraculously as I sat bewildered as to how I would reunite with my friends near the end of the final interrogation, as I looked up, they were walking by searching for me. A few weeks later, I returned back to

Harlem grateful than ever for the constant grace and mercy the

universe had provided throughout all these incidents. I began to

tread even more lightly in order to not place myself in harm's

way.

Upon writing this memoir, a desire has been created within me

to send a message both those born into and outside of the Trap.

Most importantly, to those Born into The Trap, the likelihood of

escaping will become much greater once you remove the self-

made obstacles which block your freedom. To those who are

born outside of the Trap, I would like for them to use my life

story to gain an understanding as well as empathy for the sheer

amount of pure luck and determination required for an individual

to escape the extremely well-designed societal trap unscathed.

<u>Ten Trap Commandments</u>

The path taken to escape the Trap was filled with sinkholes, quicksand, landmines, and trap doors. At every turn, it seemed the road to freedom would come to an end. Although the road seemed bleak, I devised an escape based on the experiences of those who came before me.

From an early age, I began plotting how I would escape the Trap. I vowed never to take the same path, which continued to cause so many to remain stuck in the Trap forever. I began by analyzing why families who lived in these conditions for generations either didn't want to or were incapable of escaping. My analysis led me to create a mental list of commandments of things I would adhere to while living in the Trap which would lead to my exit.

Trap Commandment #1—Never fall in love with the Trap.

I equated this to a young slave falling in love with the plantation. Can you imagine the young slave feeling loyal to the very plantation which caused such trauma to his life?

While I had many unforgettable experiences in the projects where I grew up, I was also perplexed by the amount of loyalty people in my community had to a place that caused so much stress on their mental and physical stability. Ever since I can remember, I've always seemed to gravitate towards improvement. I chose to hang out on 142nd Street and 8th Avenue in Harlem because this seemed to be the place where I could see more symbols of success when the fancy cars passing by headed to the famed Rucker Tournament on 155th Street and 8th Avenue.

I would always envision living in a place where there wasn't urine in public spaces and mailboxes weren't broken; a place safe enough where the food delivery man would bring your food to your door. Dealing with these unusual circumstances would often anger me, thereby providing the mental fuel I

needed to maintain enough focus to escape the Trap.

Many of my friends were against venturing out of the

neighborhood, but I discovered each time I ventured out I gained

a small but important sense of freedom. I would often be the one

to suggest doing activities outside of the neighborhood. I

yearned to get out of the *plantation* as much as possible.

The project to plantation analogy isn't far-fetched. When

I ventured out of my neighborhood, I noticed far less of a police

presence. In the projects, however, police officers were the

overseers, seemingly constantly keeping us in our place.

The food outside of the projects was far healthier, and

the air was fresher. During the 1990s there was a program called

The Fresh Air Fund which sent kids from low-income

communities to the countryside of upstate New York during the

summer. The Fresh Air Fund was aptly named because it

provided kids such as me a much-needed relief from the

suffocation we experienced due to the stresses of living in the Trap. It is amazing how different the air quality was between neighborhoods a mere three miles apart.

I can recall seeing their commercials and wanting to apply but never feeling the need to ask my parents. Perhaps it was because I participated in my own Fresh Air Fund by frequently venturing off the *plantation* so often.

Although I frequently ventured away from my neighborhood, it still managed to maintain a stronghold on me. From the ages of eleven to twenty-three years old, I would temporarily break my addiction to hanging out on the corner and subsequently relapse. I often questioned why I was unable to break my addiction to hanging on my block all day, but the answer would never come.

During the New York City Blackout of 2003, I was able to finally break my addiction once and for all. On this warm summer day, the entire northeastern United States was suffering a power outage, and after I came home from school, I found myself yet again hanging out on 142nd Street and 8th Avenue. Naturally, there were hundreds of people hanging outside due to the lack of air conditioning on this warm summer night. Up until this night, the longest period I had broken my addiction to the block was for six months. Initially, the camaraderie was good due to the excitement of the blackout. However, I soon had an epiphany which would forever break my attachment to the corner.

It was ironic that this epiphany happened on a day where my hanging on the corner all day would have been justified. After about an hour on the corner, I realized I hadn't even checked to make sure my mom was safe. The feeling of disappointment in myself was immense. After beginning to feel increasingly ashamed, I walked up to the block to my building. As I entered It was pitch black, but luckily, I lived on the second floor and was able to navigate my way to my apartment rather quickly. Upon entering my apartment, I embraced my mom and found that she had prepared a meal and was keeping it warm

with candles she kept in case of an emergency.

Her love truly touched me, and I was amazed by her
foresight.

Simultaneously, I felt immense guilt for not coming to

check on her sooner. This guilt allowed me to finally understand

the insanity of my infatuation with hanging on the block. It put in

perspective that I needed to focus on the people and things in

my life that truly matter instead of the corner which was there

before me and will be there long after I'm gone.

After this day, I held fast to my resolution to never stand

on the corner again. Although I loved the people in my

neighborhood, I could no longer be brainwashed into loving

living under harassment from the police, periods of no heat

during the winter, human waste in the elevators and staircases,

and just overall substandard living conditions. Up until this point,

it seemed every time I progressed in my life, and I would also

suffer a setback. Once I gave up my addiction to the block, I noticed my life rapidly improving, and for the first time, I began to feel totally free.

Trap Commandment #2—Refrain from lusting after material things that have no value.

Being born into the Trap caused many people to feel a sense of inadequacy. The byproduct of the inadequacy was a subconscious lust for material things to make us feel we weren't poor. During the mid-1990s aspirational hip hop introduced the trap to many designer fashion labels, champagne, and the overall finer things in life. Seeing the visuals of Versace shirts, yachts, foreign cars, and mansions created a lust in me, which wasn't previously there. These visuals certainly opened my eyes to the finer things' life has to offer but simultaneously caused me to feel if I didn't acquire them by the age of twenty-one, I was destined to be a failure. These constant urges for acquiring material items caused far too many of us in the Trap to risk our freedom for a pair of sneakers and a gold chain.

I used to think having Air Jordan's and a gold chain was living it up. My item of choice was Timberland boots, which at the time cost about one hundred and twenty dollars. These boots provided such a huge boost to my self-esteem. Every time I accumulated one hundred and twenty dollars; my addiction almost automatically led me to purchase a pair. Naturally, over time, my lust for these boots faded as I was introduced to the Gore-Tex ASOLO and Vasquez ski boots worn by Jay-Z in his music video for the song, *Dead Presidents*. Although a clear majority of us had never seen a ski slope, we still loved the status symbol owning a pair of these provided.

An example of this status symbol came to light while hanging out on my block. As I was standing next to my friend who was sitting on a crate as we often did during the summer, I inadvertently stomped my foot on the ground leading him to notice I had on a pair of these highly sought after ASOLO boots. He immediately praised me for owning a pair by stating, "I see you, my nigga. You gettin' a lotta money out here."

Throughout the 1990s in Harlem, this was a common response to wearing new name brand items. Hearing this constantly was almost like a drug and made me feel extremely successful; however, there was one small problem. Unbeknownst to him, I was only on the block that night because I couldn't even afford to take my girlfriend to the movies since I had spent all my money on these boots. I looked like money but was really broke.

While I was indeed happy to have the ASOLO boots, I realized that night, it is far better to spend my money on life experiences rather than expensive clothes. I surmised if I could have refrained from purchasing the ASOLO boots, I would still have two hundred and fifty dollars in my pocket instead of on my feet.

This subtle eye-opening interaction changed my outlook with regard to fashion. Up until this day I was under the assumption that if someone had on fancy clothes, they must have money, now I could see clearly if this weren't true in my case then it must be untrue for many others. In addition, in my neighborhood, many of the best-dressed people would often be the same individuals asking to borrow money.

My reprogramming was completed on a warm summer day in the Chelsea wholesale district of Manhattan where people would travel by the busload from far and wide to purchase name brand counterfeit clothing and accessories. My brother happened to be a street vendor who sold electronics and accessories. I would often join him when he restocked his inventory — my first time witnessing these caravans of buses that came from as far as South Carolina was amazing. Many of these individuals were here to resell the goods, but many others were purchasing purely for themselves. Prior to this moment, I certainly understood the appetite my community had for fashion; however, this truly magnified it. People were scrambling in and out of warehouses with five or six bags a piece. As I sat in my brother's car witnessing the shopping frenzy, I happened to look across the street and noticed there was a flea market sale going on in the park. There was immediately a glaring contrast regarding who was shopping at the warehouses versus the flea market. Once again, I analyzed the difference between what I was witnessing. The demographic makeup of those who were shopping at the warehouses was almost one hundred percent African American while those shopping across the street at the flea market were practically one hundred percent Caucasian. As I analyzed further, I could see a majority of those who were shopping at the flea market wore somewhat rundown clothes and appeared to be locals of the expensive Chelsea area. The average sales price for an apartment was nine hundred thousand dollars, and the average rent was twenty-six hundred dollars per month. I couldn't resist the urge to verbalize my observations to my brother and stated, "See how all the people who really have money are shopping at the flea market?"

My brother seemed to have a light bulb moment also but kept his sentiments internalized. I rapidly concluded the reason the Caucasians could afford to live in the expensive Chelsea neighborhood was they didn't spend a large portion of their money on material things. It appeared they valued the peace of

mind living in Chelsea afforded them more than the false

temporary feeling material items would bring. It was at this very

moment where I stood fast to the ***second trap commandment***.

Trap Commandment #3—Make robberies your last resort.

My commitment to the second Trap Commandment

greatly influenced the third Trap Commandment.   I vowed

never to commit robberies unless I was truly left with no other

option. As with the other commandments, there was an incident

tied to me, holding steadfast to my new commandment.

During the summer of 1996, as we did for the previous

two summers, we were committing armed robberies of

teenagers who worked for the summer youth program. The

summer youth participants were paid bi-weekly from June

through September with each check increasing slightly

throughout the summer. The maximum check a summer youth

program worker would receive was about three hundred dollars.

Our lust for material things was once again, causing us to risk our freedom every two weeks for three hundred dollars. Unfortunately, our two summers of success came to an end on an August afternoon. Our perceived success gave us false confidence, which led to the incarceration of two of my friends. Feeling content with the money, we accumulated this day caused me to suggest that we quit and head back to our neighborhood. My two cohorts refused and continued the robbery spree.

Several minutes prior to my suggestion, we had an intense stare down with undercover detectives who seemed to be looking for suspects. As we were walking down 127th Street between 7th and 8th Avenue, a car filled with undercover detectives slowly drove through the block. I vividly recall the thirty-second stare down with the detective in the driver's seat. I stared into the bald-headed hulking detective's piercing green eyes and noticed he had one arm and leg hanging out the driver side door. I somehow managed to remain calm even though I expected the undercover cops to jump out and attempt to arrest us. The car slowly began to come to a stop. My nervousness

caused me to crack a smile. It is my belief this smile aided in

making the detectives believe we could not possibly be the

suspects they were looking for. Nonetheless, the detectives

continued down the block, and I retreated as fast I could back to

my block, suggesting we cease our activity for the day. Rather

than walk back on this beautiful summer day, I chose to take the

train.

By the time I reached my block twenty minutes later,

word had already traveled that my two accomplices had been

arrested, subsequently receive two-year jail sentences in

Spofford, New York's version of juvenile prison. Upon hearing the

news of my close call, I heard my inner voice ask me, "What the

fuck are you doing this for?"

Since I fully understood that I didn't need to participate in

these robberies, I answered myself, "I don't know."

As absurd as these summer youth robberies were, we

often robbed Chinese food delivery men, once again risking

our freedom for less than fifty dollars while also making life

more difficult for the law-abiding citizens who would benefit

from the luxury of having their food delivered directly to their

apartment just as in the more peaceful neighborhoods. It was

at this point; I realized what I was doing was illogical and

cemented my commitment to the Third Trap Commandment

never to commit robberies unless I was truly left with no other

option.

Trap Commandments #4 and #5—Make selling drugs your last resort + Honor your ancestors by staying out of shackles.

Upon my friends' release from Spofford a few years later,

they returned to the neighborhood with intriguing stories of their

experiences in the juvenile jail. Even before they shared their

tales, they were already welcomed back to the neighborhood as

heroes. The stories only added more stripes to their hood status.

Around this same time, a few individuals were fortunate

enough to complete college and return to the neighborhood as well. I quickly noticed a surprisingly glaring difference in the

reception of those who returned home from college versus those

who returned home from jail. It was amazing to witness the

admiration for those returning from prison was far greater than

for those returning home from college. Later in life, as I achieved

financial success and began residing in affluent neighborhoods, I

would notice banners placed all over entire communities to

recognize the achievement of high school graduates committing

to a particular college. This was in stark contrast to the fashion in

which educational accomplishments were acknowledged in the

trap. In my opinion, college graduates should have received

greater admiration since they represented a symbol of success

for the rest of us. Ironically, I believe most of us in the

neighborhood secretly viewed them as failures since they went

to college and returned to a life still stuck in the Trap.

The college graduates returned to the Trap, looking

refreshed. They often had obtained their driver's licenses and

had great stories of their time on campus. Despite these facts we still mostly viewed the college experience as a waste of time

since it didn't immediately free them from the Trap.

On the contrary, the jail stories consisted of fights,

scheming, and a sense of becoming a man. Naturally, as we all

absorbed which path was most admired, most of us became

misguided secretly and sometimes overtly by the intrigues of the

prison experience. When an individual would describe either

themselves or someone we knew recently being arrested rather

than having an inflection in their voice, which pointed towards

sadness, it would most often point towards a sense of honor. The

more these conversations occurred, the less my brain could

comprehend how there could possibly be any honor in being

locked in a cage while being told when you can eat, when to

wake up, and when to go to sleep.

It became obvious to me; we were being bamboozled into

a false ideology. As I analyzed the backgrounds of my friends'

family members, I realized many of their fathers, uncles, and

brothers had given the prison system over twenty years,

combined over two or three generations. I assessed the toll the

prison system had taken on their lives, and my assessment led

me to clearly see there was no honor in going to prison unless it

was absolutely necessary. I would quietly listen to their stories of

how much money was accumulated from their drug capers and

robberies. However, 99.9 percent of the time all the money was

long gone, and there was nothing to show for all the time spent

in prison. It was as if they essentially committed crimes for free.

Upon hearing street tales of my friend's father making

one hundred fifty thousand dollars prior to receiving a ten-year

jail sentence, I calculated even if he netted one hundred fifty

thousand dollars from committing this crime, that would average

a salary of fifteen thousand dollars per year, he would be making

less than minimum wage. One could make more money over the

long term by staying out of prison and working at Home Depot

for twelve dollars an hour.

It was at this pivotal moment I merged the advice my brother

gave me about selling drugs as a last resort, and my duty to stay out of prison. Merging these two caused me to enact my *fourth Trap Commandment to sell drugs only as a last resort* and the *fifth Trap Commandment I shall honor my ancestors who were slaves by never voluntarily being placed in shackles.*

Trap Commandment #6—Take advantage of the benefits of the Trap.

A byproduct of maintaining my commitment to my fourth and fifth Trap

Commandments was the ability to buy time to figure out a plan to escape the Trap. While numerous friends were incarcerated, I was working at Home Depot accumulating the currency needed to facilitate my escape. My best friend was serving a five-year jail sentence, and during the first two years of his sentence, I accumulated roughly twenty thousand dollars in savings at the age of twenty-three.

The ability to save this amount of money was rooted in my sixth Trap Commandment. I vowed to take advantage of the low financial cost of being born into the Trap. Ever since I was young,

I realized life for those born into the Trap was rigged against us, and it was my duty to escape without taking any real punishment from society. The method of taking little punishment from the rigged society was centered around earning money legally. I knew of only one or two other people my age who amassed twenty-thousand-dollars in savings without an inheritance., lawsuit, or Illegal activity. This fact made me aware that, barring me being murdered by someone, the odds were extremely high that I would indeed escape the Trap.

Trap Commandment #7—Avoid violence as much as possible.

While it wasn't always easy to avoid conflict in the Trap, avoiding being seen for long periods of time by not standing on the corner seemed to help. This methodology of excessive conflict avoidance was ironically the same method some of my incarcerated friends used near the final months of their prison sentences in order to assure their timely release. Adopting this methodology required walking a delicate line between avoiding conflict and not being a pushover.

My desire to escape the Trap was far greater than my concern of being perceived as a pushover. I adopted my seventh Trap Commandment to avoid inflicting or becoming a victim of violence at almost all cost.

Trap Commandment #8—Don't grow up too fast.

As the possibility of my escape from the Trap became more evident the reality of becoming a victim or a victimizer caused me to spend as many hours at work and in my apartment as possible just as my incarcerated friends spent as much time working assigned jobs in jail or in their cells near the end of their release dates. This once again confirmed for me that peace is necessary to have prosperity. The peace I fought so hard to maintain throughout my time in the Trap was complemented by my eighth Trap Commandment to refrain from growing up too fast.

This was perhaps one of the hardest commandments to abide by. The various influences, such as the sociology of the trap, music, and gangster movies, provided the fuel necessary to propel an individual towards feelings of adulthood. After my close calls with the law, it became evident that I needed to slow my life down and enjoy being a teenager. Up until the age of eleven, although I was already committing petty crime; I somewhat maintained the innocence of being a child and enjoyed being afforded everything childhood entailed. Soon after I began to immerse myself in the neighborhood, the raw images of project life drained away my innocence. I began to hear numerous stories of deceased and incarcerated drug dealers who were temporarily millionaires before the age of twenty-one. These stories coupled with the images I was being bombarded with on the television screen daily provided the propaganda which served to subconsciously lead me towards the steps which would erase portions of my childhood.

During the first few months of hanging on my block, I was introduced to perhaps the most attractive fifteen-year-old girl in my neighborhood. Although she was chronologically fifteen years old, her physique and demeanor were that of at least a twenty-one-year-old. I, on the other hand, was small for twelve years old and had little experience with females. This girl blew my mind—just a few kisses from her made me feel like I was in Heaven.

During the early 1990s, fashion was paramount. This girl owned the popular 5411 Reeboks in every color and wore tight designer jeans which would attract men of any age. As our three-month relationship progressed, I began to realize I was in way over my head. Some of the slightly older guys as well as my peers began to become jealous of me and physical altercations ensued.

Prior to this time period, I basically focused on school and playing sports; however, I now had to be concerned with taking her on dates and receiving constant questions in regard to if I engaged in sexual intercourse with her yet. I was still a virgin, and honestly knew I wasn't ready to handle all the things accompanied by sexual intercourse.

I sought to hang on to our relationship, but on a cold winter night when we were playing basketball at the local community center, a friend of mine on his way home returned to notify me that she was sitting in the park cuddling with another guy. It was as if we were headed to a rumble since about twenty of us packed up and ran to the park to assess the situation. Upon arrival, she was indeed cuddled up with the other guy, and I became enraged, yelling at her, "I always knew you were a ho."

Not only was I heated, but I was also under a lot of peer pressure. With twenty of my boys looking on, I couldn't remain calm. Fortunately, the situation didn't escalate beyond angry words that day. However, the girl's cousin heard about the names I called her and wanted to fight me.

Looking back on this situation, I now view it as a coming of age of sorts. However, at the moment, I felt I was in a situation that was more suited for an eighteen-year-old. Although the fight with her cousin never materialized, my girlfriend and I soon

parted ways a few days after the incident.

Upon taking a few months to regroup from my

heartbreak, I began dating yet another overly mature sixteen-

year-old. Ironically, she shared the same name with the

fashionista rapper Lil' Kim, who was known for rapping about

designer clothes and the finer things life has to offer. The Kim I

was dating wasn't the same person; however, for her age, she

certainly mirrored the rapper in many ways. Once again, her

body was as developed as a twenty-five-year-old, and she wore

all the latest designer fashions. The major difference between

her and my first girlfriend was that I had evidence she was

previously in a relationship with a twenty-three-year-old guy who

lived in my building. This confirmed not only did she look older;

she also had the experience to match. While they were dating, I

would hear stories of expensive items they bought each other,

sexual escapades, and incidents of domestic violence. Kim was

so attractive and desired by so many guys throughout Harlem

none of these details were able to deter me. I again was fully aware I was in over my head, but now I was determined to *man up.*

Despite her previous boyfriend being ten years older than me, I constantly strategized how I would be able to compete with all the things he was previously able to provide for her. Simultaneously, I was addicted to watching the rap videos, which depicted all the things a man should buy to keep an overly attractive woman happy. As the pressure mounted and I fell deeper in what I thought was love, I soon realized once again, and I couldn't provide the material things needed to maintain this relationship.

Lil' Kim's songs consisted of mostly aspirational and materialistic themes which sought to empower woman by assuring they receive compensation from dating.

During this time many individuals, including my girlfriend, adopted the theme of these songs into their lives.

As I struggled with how I was going to provide theses designer labels for her, I realized I needed to either sell drugs or commit a big-time robbery. Fortunately, my desire to maintain my freedom was greater than my desire to provide for her. History was yet again repeating itself. A few months into my relationship with Kim, I caught her in the park with another guy when I decided to surprise her on her block. Unlike the first girlfriend I caught cheating on me in the park, I allowed her to explain and she was able to gain my forgiveness by taking me to the back of her building, passionately grinding and kissing on me until I completely forgot I had caught her sitting on some guy's lap just a few hours earlier. About a week later, I came to my senses, realizing I had been essentially hypnotized into forgiving her and decided to end our so called relationship.

A few months passed by and we crossed paths again at the famous Skate Key roller rink in the Bronx. Many people from the hoods of New York City between the ages of sixteen and thirty would gather on Saturday nights donning their most expensive attire. My parents and sister gifted me portions of their income tax refund so I could purchase the Feathered Friend Winter coat and Parasuco Jeans Overalls which were coveted by the urban community during this era. Kim took notice of my attire, verbalizing such and regrettably was able to convince me to rekindle our relationship. Unlike the past, there was a strange urgency on her part to have sex with me. Although her urgency raised my suspicions, my eagerness to lose my virginity and earn a stripe by having sex with one of the most desired women in my area caused me to disregard them. Soon after our chance meeting at Skate Key, our urgencies aligned, and we finally had sex. Since she was far more experienced than me, the encounter was brief but provided me a sense of euphoria, nonetheless. As I was riding my high of finally feeling I became an adult, she was plotting to inform me that our sole sexual encounter led to her pregnancy, even though she was currently dating someone else. She told me that she was pregnant by me and immediately needed six hundred dollars to receive an abortion. I initially panicked at the thought of being a fifteen-year-old parent, which caused me to unwittingly guarantee I would quickly provide her with any funds needed to make this situation go away.

It was at this point I was fully awakened to the consequences in relation to the opposite sex of growing up too fast. The more she pressured me for the money, the more I wished the sexual encounter never occurred. I envisioned myself having my first child at perhaps thirty years old. It was as if my life instantaneously fast forwarded fifteen years. I was terrified and aware I couldn't allow my mom to find out.

I consulted my dad for advice. After explaining the situation, my dad suggested I request evidence of her pregnancy. As I became more forceful with my request, she slowly began to retreat from her certainty of me impregnating her. She simultaneously decreased her initial six hundred dollars request by one hundred dollars with each week that passed. After a month of my resistance, Kim confessed that the whole story was indeed fabricated. Ironically, she sought to receive six hundred dollars from me to buy a pair of Alligator boots Lil' Kim rapped about.

Upon hearing this confession, I was furious, however looking back, I realized the influence these songs had on us both. So many of us born into the Trap--male and female--were in too much of a hurry to grow up and truly needed to adhere to the ***eighth Trap Commandment to refrain from growing up too fast.***

After this incident, I decided to stay single for the next two years to prevent any chance of impregnating anyone falsely or not, and although my desire for material things remained, I focused on taking a step back to analyze my every step.

Trap Commandment #9—Treat all women as you would want your mother or sister to be treated.

Even through my trials and tribulations with my first two girlfriends, I still maintained my respect for women. Although I called my first girlfriend out of her name due to my anger of catching her cheating on me, the subsequent confrontation reinforced the necessity of reverence towards women. This reverence continued to grow as I noticed many of my friends' mothers and sisters were the key factors which made a living in the Trap more bearable. It was amazing to see how mothers could manage to provide all the things we wanted with very few resources. While many of the males in the Trap were being non-productive and going to prison, the women of the Trap were going to work and obtaining degrees. In addition to work and school, these women would often take the long bus trips upstate to visit these men in prison.

My three sisters were instrumental in keeping me from becoming immersed in street life. There were times my sisters would come down the block to yank me off the corner when they deemed I was out too late. The fierce pace of their walk always allowed me to see them coming long before they reached me. Their efforts were both valiant and unsuccessful, but nonetheless, they never relented. Between the love I received from the women in my family, the calming effect I witnessed women have on even the most hardened males in my neighborhood, and often receiving information from women which prevented me from bodily harm such as the incident described earlier in the St. Nicholas housing projects, I adopted the **ninth Trap Commandment to have the utmost reverence for Women**.

Throughout my travels in the city via bus and train, I would observe the idiosyncrasies of women. My analysis led me to conclude the women who lived outside of the Trap appeared more beautiful and feminine not because they were, but because they appeared more relaxed and carefree. It would always disappoint me to see a woman in the Trap deteriorate from being the most beautiful girl anywhere at the age of sixteen into a hardened, physically far less attractive grown woman a mere ten years later. While most women maintain their stellar looks well into their forties in most cases, the Trap seemed to have a unique ability to strip women of their innate debonair nature

causing them to be labeled "washed up," as we called it in the

Trap.

 Although I don't have scientific evidence, I witnessed my ex-

girlfriend go from debonair as a teen to washed up as a young

adult back to debonair after moving out of the Trap to Atlanta,

Georgia. After returning to New York City to visit her sister in the

River Park Towers community in the Highbridge section of the

Bronx, she received endless compliments about how her skin was

glowing and how young she looked. Perhaps her resurgence

stemmed from being in an environment where women are

granted reverence for the most part. Once she got a taste of this

healthy environment, she vowed to never return to the days

when constant harassment and being called a bitch or a hoe was

a part of merely walking to and from the neighborhood store.

 These are behaviors I never witnessed my father exhibit onto

my mother. I believe this was a major factor in allowing her to

maintain her natural style and grace. Although we witnessed

plenty of chaos and disrespect outside of our home, my five

siblings and I received the maximum love and affection within

the walls of our three-bedroom project apartment.   It is my

belief that the harmony we were privileged to have aided in

preventing all my siblings from ever entering the prison system

which has almost guaranteed our children will inherit an

improved standard of living than was afforded to us.

Trap Commandment #10—Each Generation Should do better than the previous

My realization that other races often are born better off

than their parents led me to the tenth Trap Commandment to

ensure my children will begin life in a better financial position

than me.   I would often wonder where the term "race" derived

from. Although we were taught it was synonymous with

"species," I rejected this notion. Instead, I viewed the word race

in a literal sense. This mentality caused me to look at life as a relay race in which I needed to pass the baton cleanly to the next generation with little to no room for error.

The setbacks the African race suffered from slavery were tremendous, and I attributed our lagging behind other races to us, not having the opportunity to pass the baton generation after generation in the relay race of life. I would compare my immigrant parents' standard of living in their native country of Haiti to the standard of living they now had in the United States. It was clear they were running the race at a good enough pace, which would allow my siblings and me a good start once we received the baton from them.

In contrast, there seemed to be strategically placed obstacles on the racetrack, which were meant to prevent African Americans from even competing in the race of life. Throughout history, there have been several socio-economic factors implemented which have caused Africans throughout the world to lag behind. Slavery was the initial obstacle necessary to rig the race of life. If laps on a racetrack were years, it allowed other races a four hundred -lap head start throughout the world. Not only did slavery rig the race, it completely froze Africans in time as other races sprinted around the track.

Once the Caucasians were far enough ahead, slavery was abolished; however, the extreme disadvantage was never acknowledged as evidenced by the absence of reparations. All other ethnicities who suffered human rights abuses throughout modern times were granted an economic boost to return them to their rightful position on the racetrack of life. Perhaps Africans weren't granted the same boost due to the fear of them rapidly catching up?

This observation led me to question why the Caucasians in South Africa deemed it necessary to implement the obstacle of Apartheid to restrict the advancements of Black South Africans. I have always been perplexed why white supremacists across the world who viewed themselves as naturally superior to Africans constantly needed to place obstacles aimed at suppressing other races.

In America, during the 1980s and 1990s, the obstacle placed was the strategic placement of crack into African American communities. This seemed to be the easiest way to drop the baton due to the fact it was so easy to be arrested for selling even the smallest quantity thereby acquiring a criminal record, receiving a long prison sentence and being disqualified from competing in the race of life.

We were tricked into believing picking up the drugs would accelerate us on the track, but a clear majority of the time caused us to drop the baton and fall behind forever. While other races were mass producing doctors, lawyers, and other high-income professionals, African Americans were unknowingly mass-producing prisoners due to the drug trade. Any chance of narrowing the income gap between races evaporated during this period. It is my estimation that a minimum of twenty-five years

of successfully passing the baton is necessary for African

Americans to have even the slightest chance at closing the gap.

It is imperative that Africans worldwide are cognizant of the next

obstacle history is placing on the racetrack of life far before we

are irretrievably damaged yet again.

www.ingramcontent.com/pod-product-compliance
Lightning Source LLC
Chambersburg PA
CBHW031054250726

48655CB00004B/1435